T0129422

Discovering
Angels

How to Invite Angels into Your Life for
Peace, Tranquility, and Personal Change

Pamela Landolt, M.Msc.

BALBOA.
PRESS
A DIVISION OF HAY HOUSE

Balboa Press books may be ordered through booksellers or by contacting:

Balboa Press
A Division of Hay House
1663 Liberty Drive
Bloomington, IN 47403
www.balboapress.com
1 (877) 407-4847

Because of the dynamic nature of the Internet, any web addresses or
links contained in this book may have changed since publication and
may no longer be valid. The views expressed in this work are solely those
of the author and do not necessarily reflect the views of the publisher,
and the publisher hereby disclaims any responsibility for them.

The author of this book does not dispense medical advice or prescribe the use
of any technique as a form of treatment for physical, emotional, or medical
problems without the advice of a physician, either directly or indirectly. The
intent of the author is only to offer information of a general nature to help
you in your quest for emotional and spiritual well-being. In the event you use
any of the information in this book for yourself, which is your constitutional
right, the author and the publisher assume no responsibility for your actions.

Any people depicted in stock imagery provided by Getty Images are
models, and such images are being used for illustrative purposes only.
Certain stock imagery © Getty Images.

Print information available on the last page.

ISBN: 978-1-5043-9779-7 (sc)
ISBN: 978-1-5043-9778-0 (hc)
ISBN: 978-1-5043-9777-3 (e)

Library of Congress Control Number: 2018901753

Balboa Press rev. date: 03/21/2018

contents

list of exercises

This book is dedicated to my two sons, Ryan and Sean,
whose presence in my life has been and always will be
among my greatest blessings.
Thank you for sharing life with me and
for giving me the opportunity to experience
the unconditional love a mother has for a child.
Love You Forever.

*"The best and most beautiful things in the world
cannot be seen nor even touched,
but just felt in the heart."*

-- Helen Keller
American author, *The Story of My Life*
(1st edition 1904)

acknowledgments

This book has been made possible through the love I have experienced from all the angels in my life: my family, friends, and mentors, and of course, those high-vibrational beings you will learn about here. In some way, each has been part of my growth process, and the person I am today has much to do with learning to trust what I see, hear, sense, and know from the angels.

I thank Doreen Virtue for sharing so much through her books, cards, and classes. I began reading Doreen's books in the 1990s, when angels were still a mystery to me. I have since read most of Doreen's books and am grateful to her for sharing with me and millions of others her knowledge, wisdom, and guidance in learning to trust the messages the angels provide. Doreen was the first to introduce me to the angels and to guide me as I began my journey.

I am extremely grateful for author and teacher of angel healing and alchemy, Angela McGerr, who came into my life at a time when sadness and desperation were knocking at my door. Instead of darkness, I was greeted by the light of the angels that stood behind that door. I was presented with Angela's *Love and Light Angel Cards,* a beautiful deck of angel cards with surreal paintings of images that drew me in, comforted me, and gave me hope. The accompanying book explained angels in a way I had never heard of or thought of before. I am grateful to Angela for being the vehicle the angels chose to help me on that day when, in Barnes & Noble, her book so magically found its way into my hands, my mind, and my heart.

Thank you, also, to my most dear angel mentor, Emmanuelle Pries, who, by way of synchronicity, came into my life as my teacher of Angela McGerr's angelology courses, which were my beginning of understanding that the angels have been with me my entire life. She opened my eyes and my heart and validated for me the angelic connections I didn't even realize I was experiencing. It is through Emmanuelle's knowledge, compassion, expression, love, light, mentorship, and friendship that I am able to bring to you this learning guide. It is with deep love and admiration that I acknowledge energy healer, teacher, and vibrational expert, Emmanuelle, in love, light, and angel sparkles forever.

I would like to honor two dear friends with whom I share a special connection along this spiritual journey. To Carolyn Joseph, for the numerous energy healings we've exchanged, always when most needed. Our spiritual growth and friendship have taken us many places, Lily Dale being among some of the most treasured experiences shared. I thank her for being my dear friend and being present in my life. To Barbara Lynch, who has been my rock in times of need, my advisor in times of change. She encouraged me through all phases of my healing and angelic endeavors, including participating in case studies as I worked toward achieving certifications. Throughout the years and for so many projects, including this book, she has provided feedback, perspective, and encouragement. We have shared good times, sad times, growing children, and empty nests, but some of the most fun times shared were "girlfriend time meetings" at Saint Francis Hospital! I thank her for her friendship, and for being my angel in disguise.

I'd also like to acknowledge one of my oldest friends, Linda Schuyler Ford, whose friendship is undoubtedly, and happily, lasting a lifetime. Look how far we've come on our life journeys—journeys we started together at about age five.

A special note of appreciation goes out to Linda, herself a storyteller and educator, for reviewing the final copy of this manuscript and again to Barbara Lynch, whose help throughout the process of creating *Discovering Angels* has been invaluable. It is with sincere gratitude that I acknowledge you both for helping me bring this book to life.

To all the angelic energies who have come to me, helped me understand, and provided me with their knowledge to share, I am honored to tell your stories and remain forever and always grateful.

Lastly, I want to thank *you*, the reader of this book, for allowing me to become part of your journey as you venture out into the world of angels. May you always know the angels are near.

introduction

Angels are all around us. They are our protectors, our guides, our healers, and our friends, but above all, they are here to love us. I am not a scholar on the subject of angels. I do not claim to have studied the *historical* or *theological* concepts of angels. I don't claim to be an expert on all there is to know about the world of angels. I am just an average, ordinary person with an ordinary life, who has been a receiver of angelic assistance as far back as I can remember—even unknowingly, when I didn't remember.

I say unknowingly because at the time of several encounters, I was completely unaware of the power of the angels and how fortunate I was to have them protecting and guiding me. I did often wonder about my mother's maiden name, Cherubino. I fantasized as a child that we were somehow connected to the angels you think about on Valentine's Day, the cherubs, better known as those baby angels shooting their arrows into the hearts of lovers. When I was a child, I always seemed to have a special feeling when I saw pictures or statues of angels or heard church music, which gave me a light and comforting feeling in my heart. I know now that that feeling was love-energy, the energy of the angels. But it wasn't until I was much older that I realized the important role the angels have played and are still playing in my life. I recall a story my mother told me many years ago. She called it a miracle; I now know it was Archangel Michael coming to the rescue.

When I was two years old, my family moved to an army base in Germany where my father was assigned. My mother, a dance teacher, began teaching in a school gymnasium, which was in the basement of the building. While my mother taught, I would sit on a little child-sized chair in the corner of the gym. One day, while my mother was teaching, there were boys playing basketball outside. Their basketball hit the window, and glass came crashing down right where I was sitting. As this happened, my mother ran over to me, so afraid I was covered in glass, but much to her amazement, the shattered glass formed a complete, symmetrical circle right around me and the chair I was sitting on. There was not one piece, not even one speck of glass on me or on the chair. My mother couldn't believe her eyes. With tears rolling down her cheeks, she picked me up, saying "It's a miracle. It's a miracle."

She told me this story when I was in my twenties, and I agreed that it had to be a miracle. Then one day, over a decade later, I realized that not only was it a miracle, but it was Archangel Michael, angel of strength and protection, bearer of sword and shield, who protected me that day as he placed his shield over my head so that the shattered glass formed a complete, symmetrical circle around me. I remember the day I realized this; it brought tears to my eyes while simultaneously bringing warmth and love to my heart, and a memory of those feelings I used to have as a child.

Although I have since read a considerable amount about angels from such renowned authors as Doreen Virtue and Angela McGerr, most of my relationship-building with the angels has taken place when I began to notice angels are near. But you don't know what you don't know, so for a very long time, I was receiving messages and didn't even realize it.

One other note before you delve into this material. Various religious traditions have different names, spellings, and classifications for the angels. For example, variations of the Archangel Camael's name include Chamuel, Khamael and

Camniel. Archangel Gabriel is not referred to as an archangel in the Bible, but is in the Book of Enoch and other post testament texts. If you come across a name or spelling of an angel that is different from what you have previously known, please don't get hung up on this and just refer to the angel in the way that is comfortable for you. This is a nondenominational book to introduce you to the angels and help you learn how to communicate with them. Keep your focus pure and uncritical, and always work in a way that is comfortable for you. You will undoubtedly be amazed by the love and guidance you experience from the angels.

Everyone has the ability to receive messages from the angels. The angels want us to be able to recognize them. But like most any other skill, it takes practice. Learning to communicate with the angels is no different. First, you must be willing to notice, then to practice noticing, then to learn how to interpret what you notice, and then finally, to trust the messages you interpret. Before you know it, you too will be communing with the angels, receiving help and guidance in all areas of your life.

It is with great pleasure and extreme gratitude that I share with you my interpretations of the world of angels and hope that through this book you will learn to form your own relationship with them. One of the most important thoughts to keep in mind is that everyone can communicate with the angels. One person's interpretation is not the only or "right" way to communicate with those of the angelic world. Each relationship is different and unique to the person and his or her angels. This guide will help you learn some of the basics of how to see, hear, feel, sense, or know that the angels are near. As a result of this new knowledge, when speaking to the angels, either out loud or in silent thought, you will be able to recognize the angelic signs or symbols the angels have uniquely provided to let you know they are near. When you read through this book and practice the exercises, you will begin to understand the messages your angels intend you to have. This may not happen right away, but don't be discouraged; just keep practicing, releasing any fear or resistance you may have, and allow the angels into your heart. Before you know it, you will be communing with the angels.

This is a self-guided book designed to be read and practiced at your own pace. No two people are alike, and therefore, know that your own experience will differ from that of another. No matter how quickly you learn or how long it takes, be comfortable with the fact that you are going at exactly the right pace for you. Let the angels be your guide. It may be helpful for you to record your personal experiences in the journal section provided at the back of the book. This will help you to remember the results of your exercises, and as time goes on, you will be able to look back to see how you've progressed.

The exercises in this book will help you recognize, connect with, and strengthen your relationship with the angels. Do them as often as you like, and know that the more you practice, the easier it will become to connect and communicate with the angels. The book contains several guided meditations to help you connect with the angels. No prior meditation experience is needed. All you need to do is to sit in a comfortable position where you won't be disturbed for ten to fifteen minutes, and relax. Read the meditation first; then close your eyes and visualize what you just read, or, you can record yourself reading the meditation out loud and then listen to your own voice guiding you through the meditation. If your mind happens to drift off in another direction, acknowledge it and then bring your attention back to the meditation image. Do this as often as you need to. Eventually, you will be able to go through the meditation without much distraction. Practice and you'll get it.

From this book, you will learn to recognize signs that the angels are near. You will be introduced to the Sacred Seven: these are the archangels charged with ruling the seven days of the week. You will learn about the zodiac and nature angels: about their attributes, how to call upon them, and how they can help you. You will discover that one of the Sacred Seven is your primary guardian angel. This is your birth guardian, the angel that was with you on the day you were born, who will remain your guardian throughout your life. In the pages that follow, you will be working with the four "clairs" (clairaudience, clairvoyance, clairsentience and claircognizance), learning the difference between them, methods of practice to strengthen your "clair" abilities, and determining which "clair" is easiest for you to receive your angelic messages. Most find they gravitate toward one, although with practice, you can develop all four.

Please realize that developing your relationship with the angels may take time, so be easy with yourself, relax into the process of allowing, and most of all, have fun!

chapter 1

angels all around us

Angels have been part of religious and spiritual belief systems since ancient times, and numerous references are found within religious texts. While associated with organized religions, angels are nondenominational and want to help your personal growth and development regardless of your religious beliefs or affiliations. Angels do not have genders and may be referred to in either masculine or feminine terms. Refer to the angels with "he" or "she" as you personally sense them, but do not allow gender terms to sidetrack you.

The word *angel* represents a group of high-vibrational beings with frequencies greater than those that our five senses are generally able to interpret, see, hear, smell, touch, or taste. Angel energy is love energy, and the angels are love. Angels love everyone and everything, unconditionally. Think for a moment how *love* feels. How does it feel to you? Does love give you a warm, comforting, soothing feeling? Does it give you a feeling of being secure, blissful, happy, and joyful? Does love expand your heart, make you smile, and make your heart smile? If you've ever experienced love of any kind—whether romantic love, the love of a parent for a child, the love of a pet, love for nature, love for the arts, or anything that gives you that special feeling—you have experienced the magic of the angels, because angels *are love*.

Based on having experienced love in some form, can you recall ever being able to see, hear, touch, smell, or taste love? Think about this for a moment. Have you ever experienced love through one of your five senses? You might recall feeling love when you petted your dog or cat, or when you gazed at a majestic scene. But was it the *action* of petting through the sense of touch that caused the feelings of love? Was it the *action* of gazing through the sense of sight that caused the feelings of love? In both instances, the action was not the cause but the vehicle through which the angels helped you experience the feelings of love that were felt in your heart—or maybe throughout your whole body. Think about the last time you smelled the sweet fragrance of a flower or heard music that calmed you or made your soul sing. These are all ways that the angels are getting our attention. Although the angels hold a higher vibrational frequency than our five senses can pick up on, they are always finding ways to let us know they are with us. Being a catalyst for love is one way you know the angels exist within you.

Angels are ethereal, formless, celestial beings of light that hold, vibrate, and emit the frequency of pure, unconditional love. Simply put, angels are love, love holds an angelic vibration, and that vibration is unconditional love. The angels are constantly looking for ways to get our attention. They focus on our good attributes and are nonjudgmental. Because they are pure love and light energy not bound by physical bodies, they are ever-present and able to be at many places at the same time. So never worry that your request is too small and not important enough for the angels' attention, or that it's seemingly too large. The angels are always ready to assist you. The only requirement for receiving angelic assistance and guidance is that you ask them for their help or guidance. This is because as humans, we have free will. Angels cannot interfere with our free will choices and must wait patiently to be summoned by us for their assistance. There is one exception to this rule, which will be discussed later.

You might be wondering, "In what ways can the angels help?" The answer is, "In *all* ways." You see, the angels are our protectors, our healers, our messengers, our guides, our advisors, and our friends, all without limits. They want to help us in every aspect of our lives. Some angels have specialized areas of focus. If we learn them, our requests can then be more focused, and this may expedite the help and guidance we receive. When you call to the angels, if you call generically, you will also get the help you need. But by calling upon the angel who specializes in your type of problem or concern, you are maximizing the energy of your request, and therefore, the angelic guidance you receive will most likely be accelerated.

How do we know the angels are near? The angels are around us all the time and are constantly trying to get our attention. How do they try to get our attention? They give us signs, but we need to know what to look for. Have you ever found a feather on the ground? Finding feathers is one way the angels are telling us they are near. Another sign is finding coins on the ground, especially pennies and dimes (or the equivalent in other currencies). Fragrances seemingly coming from nowhere are also signs that the angels are near. (A waft of the floral scent of rose, lily, or geranium is common.) Other ways to recognize the angels are near include the feeling of tingling, goose bumps, and a slight breeze when the air is otherwise still, or seeing sparkles or flashes of light for no apparent reason. Angels come to us in ways that are very personal to us as individuals. There are no wrong ways to perceive the angels, which you will see as you begin to work on and develop your own relationship with them. Begin to notice signs that the angels are near, and jot them down in your journal. Have you found a penny lately? (Heads or tails doesn't matter.) Jot it down with the date. Have you found a feather lately? Jot it down. This way, you'll be able to track your progress and see that, without a doubt, the angels *are near.*

chapter 2

everyone has a guardian angel

The angels love assisting you in all areas of your life. They are around you all the time. Everyone has a guardian angel. Actually, everyone has at least two guardian angels. Here we will discuss your primary angel, your birth guardian. At the moment you were born, your birth guardian angel entered your life and has remained with you. This special angel watches over you, loves you, and guides you. This is the angel that sends you the most signs and is most persistent in trying to let you know you are not alone.

Your primary guardian angel is one of seven archangels charged with governing the specific day of the week you were born. These angels, known as the Sacred Seven, each hold vibrations for certain aspects of life. In addition to ruling over the days of the week, they are associated with specific colors, musical notes, and crystals or stones, each holding certain healing vibrations that help you in your times of need. Knowing these associations is not necessary for receiving angelic guidance, but it does have advantages. Having this knowledge will help you to call upon the angel that carries the vibration closest to the problem or concern you are trying to take care of. This will expedite the guidance or solution as well as help you develop a personal relationship with the angels, strengthening and enhancing your angelic connection. Don't worry if you need help in an area that an angel other than your guardian specializes in. In this case, you would work with that angel but ask your guardian to watch over your process. Your guardian will help to keep you on the right path, overseeing and supervising each step of the way. Think of your guardian as your angel manager. While you may receive signs from many angels letting you know they are here to help in your times of need, and they will, your primary guardian is always by your side and will direct those angels so that you are best served.

You may want to develop a special relationship not only with your guardian but with the other Sacred Seven angels as well. If you don't already know the day of the week you were born, now is a good time to look it up.

Monday's Guardian
Archangel Gabriel

If you were born on a Monday, Gabriel is your primary guardian. Gabriel can help you with your aspirations. What are your hopes and dreams? Are you confused about what you truly want out of life? Do you need clarification? A direction? Do you need encouragement to take that first step or motivation to keep going when things get tough? Gabriel is here to help.

Gabriel is associated with the energies of the moon; he can help you balance the ebb and flow of emotions and bring into harmony the feminine side of creativity and intuitiveness with the masculine side of movement and action. Regardless of our gender, we all have both a feminine and a masculine side. Harmony between the two brings into balance our right- and left-brain functions so that we can be creative, sensitive, and intuitive while taking action to bring to fruition whatever we wish to manifest in life. (Right-brain function governs the left side and feminine self of emotion, creativity, and intuition, while left-brain function governs the right side and masculine self of movement, logic, and action.)

Archangel Gabriel is also associated with the throat chakra, which is related to verbal communication. When you need to express yourself clearly, whether in one-on-one conversations or addressing large audiences, Gabriel will be there for you, especially if he is your guardian angel. Gabriel is also attuned to the sound made by the note G, which should be easy to remember (G is for Gabriel). Just hearing the tone made by the note G can bring Gabriel to your side. Holding or wearing a moonstone will also aid in your connection with Gabriel.

I asked Gabriel to give me a special message for those guided to read this book. This is the message I received for you.

> *I am Gabriel, guardian of the moon and those born on Monday. You may call upon me for guidance in areas where clarity is needed and direction is sought for any project or dream, no matter how large and no matter how small. Ask for my help and I will guide you in the direction needed for taking steps to begin, maintain, and succeed. If you experience being overwhelmed, call to me and I will ease your emotions and place in proper perspective your situation at hand. Holding a piece of my moonstone close to your heart will help calm your emotions, especially those emotions of insecurity often felt when venturing into territory unknown, as with seeking to turn your dreams into your reality. I do this all with the light of my love; all you need to do is ask. For those of whom I am guardian, I am with you always. Look for my signs; I send them often.*

Tuesday's Guardian
Archangel Camael

If you were born on a Tuesday, Camael is your primary guardian. Camael can help you any time you need the courage to move forward, especially in times where you need to take a stand on a certain issue or concern but are unsure of yourself and feel stuck, unable to move or take action. Are you lacking in self-confidence or looking for ways to improve in this area? Do you have a big moment coming up that is creating anxiety?

Camael is associated with the root chakra, which is our foundation, our security in life. It governs how we "walk around" in the world. Do you have a strong, firm foundation, or is it weak, shaky, or wobbly? Camael can help fortify your foundation, providing you with the strength and courage to take on any matters that need your attention. The color associated with the root chakra is red, and therefore, that is the color represented by Camael. Wear the color red or hold any red stone, such as garnet, ruby, or red carnelian, with the intention for Camael to be with you, and Camael will immediately be by your side. Another easy way to remember how to bring in the energies of Camael is to tone or play the musical note C—C for Camael.

When I asked Camael for a special message for you, the reader, this is what I received.

> *I am Camael, and am here to guide all who request my help. Some may seek courage or confidence, while others need comforting or security. I am here to show you where to find it all, for it is all within yourself. Think about the story of Dorothy and Oz and how hard she tried to get home; yet all it took was realizing she had the power within herself all the time. When Dorothy closed her eyes, clicked her ruby-reds, and looked within, it was in that instant, her heart's desire became her reality, and*

she was home again. I give this example, and there are so many more examples that could be given, but this will do, as looking within is the point I wish to make. I can help you with this; to seek and discover the path to your desired reality. If needed, I can also help strengthen your core foundation, which will instill the security needed for a healthy sense of self. This will give you the confidence to look within and handle any situation that comes your way. Call upon me on Tuesdays for additional strength and support.

Wednesday's Guardian
Archangel Michael

If you were born on a Wednesday, Michael is your guardian. Michael can help you any time you need strength or protection. Are you entering a situation where you find yourself uncomfortable or feel concerned for your safety? Do you have a job that requires a tremendous amount of strength, or are you a protector yourself, such as those dedicated to law enforcement or fighting fires? Call upon Michael to be with you, and he will guide you through difficult days and situations.

In addition to strength and protection, Michael is also the angel of truth and is associated with the third-eye chakra. He can help you "see" your truth, even if it is hiding behind old emotional "scripts." He can help you see the unwanted patterns and habits caused by these scripts that are blocking your ability to live your truth now. Ask Michael for help and with his sword, Michael will "cut" away the invisible strings of old scripts limiting your truth. With this shield, Michael will protect you as you release old behaviors that masqueraded as coping mechanisms; so you may see your truth. With his cloak, Michael will comfort you as tears flow safely and without self-judgment, creating space for healing; so you may feel your truth. With his love, Michael will guide you toward realizing your full potential; so you may live your truth. Michael's healing colors are blues and yellows, and stones linked to him include sapphire, turquoise, blue topaz, yellow topaz, citrine, and yellow calcite. His musical tone is the note A.

Michael's special message to you is about truth.

> *I am here to help you know your truth. Everyone has both a personal truth and a divine truth. These truths are linked together like pieces of a puzzle. At first, you may not distinguish what pieces fit where, or what relationship each piece has to another and therefore to the whole. But as you discover more pieces of your personal truth and how they fit within your life, your divine truth begins to come into focus and with this knowledge, it all becomes clear. You see, your truth laid out in scattered pieces makes it difficult to perceive your life-purpose. But once you begin sorting and restoring, you find the pieces of your personal truth and those of your divine truth fit together perfectly. Your whole picture becomes clear, and your total truth is known. I can help you put the pieces of your personal and divine truths together, as they are and forever will be energetically linked and connected to your soul growth and soul's life-purpose. Ask for my help and guidance if you wish to begin this journey.*

Before moving on to Thursday, I want to note here that it is important to ask for our angels' help because they will not interfere with our free will. As mentioned previously, there is an exception to this, and that exception is Archangel Michael. As the angel of strength and protection, Michael will come to the aid of a person, whether or not that person has called to the angels, if he or she is in a life-threatening situation and it is not his or her time for the experience. Have you ever heard stories about the "stranger" who appeared out of nowhere at the scene of a car accident, helped the victim out of the car, and then disappeared before the person was able to thank him? I know of three people who have experienced this, and there is no doubt in my mind that their "strangers" were Archangel Michael.

Thursday's Guardian
Archangel Zadkiel

If you were born on Thursday, your primary guardian is Zadkiel. Helping you identify and embrace the abundance in your life is one of Zadkiel's gifts. Do you often speak of what you don't have, what you wish you had, or what someone else has that you want? This is coming from a point of lack rather than abundance. Zadkiel can bring into your awareness *all* the abundances in your life, not just those coming from material possessions. Do you have a love in your life, close friendships, good health, a secure job, or a comfortable place to live? These are examples of where you can find abundance in your life, and the list goes on and on. If you are in need of a clearer perspective of the blessings and gifts in your life, call to Zadkiel for assistance.

He is associated with the crown chakra and shades of purple and violet. Calling to Zadkiel while wearing or holding stones of these colors, such as amethyst, charoite, or tanzanite, will bring him to you immediately, and so will hearing or toning the musical note B.

Zadkiel's message to you is about understanding abundance.

> *Call to me for help understanding that abundance comes from much more than your material possessions. Expressing gratefulness for all that*

comes into your life, knowing there is always a reason, even for the difficult situations, and there are always lessons to be learned from your experiences, provides a life of understanding, purpose and fulfillment. Likewise, persistent attention toward what is not yours, expressing blame, frustration, or anger surely keeps you stuck in a pattern of lack, and the pattern of not having continues. I can help you understand that the things that appear to be causing problems and challenges in your life are not obstacles, but rather indicators that positive change is needed. These obstacles are providing opportunities for soul lessons and growth. Once this is understood and accepted and gratitude for these experiences is expressed, abundance begins to flow. It's a cycle. The situation provides a lesson, which promotes choice, which provides opportunity for growth, which provides space for the next situation and lesson, which promotes choice, and then growth, and then space, and so on. Allow me to help you learn from this wisdom and attain this awareness. For there is great abundance in and surrounding your life, and it comes in many forms.

Friday's Guardian
Archangel Haniel

If you were born on a Friday, Haniel is the guardian who watches over you. Haniel can help in all situations of the heart, including loving and expressing love toward yourself in the form of self-appreciation. Are you someone who easily shows compassion toward others but tends to be critical of yourself? Is it easier to give love than receive love, or equally difficult to both give and receive? Do you lack self-esteem and find it hard to express joy? Whatever the reasons may be, Haniel is here to guide and teach you how to open your heart to love and how to appreciate all your unique qualities. Call upon her for help in all matters pertaining to your self-image and self-confidence, and she will lovingly assist you in making the necessary changes that will allow you to live a happy, joyful life.

Haniel is affiliated with the heart chakra and the sound made by the note F. Her colors are both pink, for giving and receiving love, and green, for healing a broken or frozen heart. To encourage Haniel's presence while calling to her, hold a pink stone, such as rose quartz, kunzite, or pink tourmaline, or a green one, such emerald, malachite, or green tourmaline; or listen to the sound of the note F.

Haniel's message to you is about healing heart.

I am the angel of compassion, and I am here to show you how to love and have compassion for yourself. The first step in true love is to love oneself. It is easier to express love than to receive it. This is because your heart is not completely open. Somewhere in your past, there was a heart-hurt, and as a defense, you closed a portion of your heart. You did this unknowingly; it was a subconscious act of protection at that time. The number and intensity of heart-hurts you have experienced determines how closed your heart is. With each hurt, the heart closes a little more and a little more. Somewhere during these times, you didn't see, or you misunderstood, the cause of the experience, which was the lesson you were being presented with. These lessons vary with each soul-person and circumstance, but to provide examples of human lessons for healing heart-hurts, there is forgiveness and often self-forgiveness, compassion as well as self-compassion, how to nurture including yourself, and how to love unconditionally beginning with yourself. These are among the highest lesson priorities at this time. However, know that the number of lessons presented are countless and are as individualized as each of you. I will guide you through your heart chakra to clear any blocks preventing you from living a joyous and fulfilled life. We will voyage on this journey together as I help you navigate through the seas of self-love and compassion. You only just need to ask.

Saturday's Guardian
Archangel Cassiel

If you were born on a Saturday, Cassiel is your guardian. Cassiel is the peacemaker, the one who brings a sense of harmony and calmness into your life. If you are like many people I know, you are constantly on the go. Life has us multitasking more than ever before. It has now become a common way of life. Do you ever wish you could be in two places at the same time? I know I do, and sometimes in three places! The result of this fast-paced life is increased stress. I know so many people who have stress-related illnesses. We really do need to take the time to stop and bring peace and harmony back into our lives. There is power in the saying "stop and smell the flowers."

Cassiel can help by guiding us toward finding creative ways to bring calmness back into our lives. This is done by working with the sacral chakra and with the note D. Cassiel's colors are black and white for balance and harmony, so stones that are beneficial to use when calling upon Cassiel include apache tears, black and white agate, and snowflake obsidian.

Cassiel's message to you is about healthy balance.

I am Cassiel and I bring to you a means of finding balance between daily responsibilities and your own true peace within. Stop and make time for yourself. Stop and find an outlet that brings calmness inward. Stop and breathe, breathe, breathe. Breathe counts of four. Inhale one-two-three-four, hold one-two-three-four, exhale one-two-three-four, and do this at least three times; twelve is best. Take time to stop and do this often during the day and it will relax you. It will clear your mind. It will help you to focus on your tasks at hand. If you are in need of bringing balance into your life, call upon me for help and guidance. Are you torn between the pressures of work-life and home-life? Is this causing you stress? Ask me to help bring peace and tranquility into your life so that you may maintain harmony and a healthy balance. Stress caused by unbalance can inflict instability and unhealthy chaos within one's physical body. Call on me to reduce this stress and rid yourself of its effect. I will help. But if nothing else, breathe.

Sunday's Guardian
Archangel Raphael

If you were born on a Sunday, your guardian is Raphael. Raphael is the angel of healing, knowledge, and masculine and feminine balance, and he can help in many ways. Look to Raphael when you are sad; he will comfort you with his healing light. As the angel of knowledge, Raphael will bring comfort and then help you understand the situation, putting it into perspective, bringing clarity to the cause of your sadness. As the angel who balances our masculine, thinking, active selves with our feminine, creative, emotional selves, once perspective is gained, Raphael will guide you toward taking the appropriate steps for uplifting your spirits.

Raphael is affiliated with the solar plexus chakra, our place of personal power. As ruler of the sun, Raphael provides us with the warmth of his golden yellow light; this is also the color affiliated with the solar plexus. Additionally, he is associated with white and the colors of the rainbow.

Call upon Raphael while holding or wearing stones of yellow, such as sunstone, yellow citrine, or yellow topaz for comfort, knowledge, and balance. To work with Raphael's healing properties, holding or wearing a clear quartz crystal or diamond will be most powerful. You may also call Raphael to you through the note E.

Raphael's message to you is about healing.

> *Call upon me when you start to feel ill or are experiencing feelings of sadness or uneasiness of any kind. I work to strengthen your immune system by balancing your chakras, which help to circumvent any illness—physical, emotional, or spiritual. Chakras are wheels of energy that spin in a vortex-like action in and out of the body, and throughout the body's non-physical fields. They are invisible to the untrained mind, but their balance is key to your health. There are seven major chakras in the center line of your body. When they are functioning correctly, you are in health; but when there is imbalance, you are susceptible to dis-comfort, dis-ease, and, if left unattended for too long, eventually disease. A hypothetical example is the feeling of anxiety. At first, it may just cause the dis-comfort of what you call butterflies in your stomach. If it is not addressed and the anxiety persists over time, you may begin to feel*

the dis-ease of pain in your abdomen. If ignored and left unattended for too long, this abdominal pain may manifest into the disease called ulcers. Energetically, this anxiety is originally caused by an imbalance of the solar plexus chakra, the chakra associated with one's personal power. I can help balance your energy field and guide you toward self-nurturing methods, such as meditation and energy movement techniques, which can help keep your chakras strong to maintain health. Work with me and a piece of clear quartz crystal for added assistance. Quartz is a most powerful tool, which will aid you in the absorption of my healing energy. A clear quartz holds all the healing color vibrations within, and because each chakra is associated with a healing color, holding or wearing a quartz will bring the associated color vibration needed, into your energy field. The healing color vibrations are red for the first or root chakra; orange for the second, sacral chakra; yellow for the third, solar plexus chakra; pink and green for the fourth, heart chakra; light blue for the fifth, throat chakra; dark blue/indigo for the sixth, third eye chakra; and violet for the seventh, crown chakra. Call upon me whenever you need help in warding off physical, emotional, or spiritual dis-comfort, or if you are just in need of a little comforting. I am here for you. For all serving in a healing profession, whether through your modern medicine fields or in one of the many energy healing modalities, I commend you and can serve in helping you to stay healthy and strong in order that you may continue your fine work. Call upon me for assistance.

chapter 3

inviting angels into your life

The first step in communing with the angels is being able to know when they are near. Now you know that the angels are always with you and, I hope, have even begun to recognize some of their signs. Have you come across any feathers, coins, unexpected wafts of fragrance, or repetition of numbers or words? Hopefully you have, but if not, don't worry, now that you're aware, you will.

The next step is to begin calling upon the angels for a specific purpose. Although the angels are around us all the time, they cannot interfere with our free will and therefore, must be invited into our lives if we want their guidance or help with a situation. To maximize the strength of your invocation, you will follow the rule of three and call the name of the angel three times. The number three is a significant number that represents creation and the initial activation key for manifesting a formation into completion. You'll find many examples of this as demonstrated in three life stages of women (maiden, mother, crone), the three phases of the moon (waxing, full, waning) or the three aspects of self (body, mind, spirit). I have found that calling the angel's name three times helps to open and complete the vibrational connection that occurs when we invoke the angels.

In addition to calling the angel's name three times, there is another rule of three you'll want to remember: "Invite, Ask, Thank." Let me explain further.

> *Invite:* Much like when we invite a friend to visit, our angels need to be invited to visit us too. It needs to be clear to the angels that our intention is for them to be present with us and help us with our situation. So invite by calling to the angels, or to a specific angel, three times.

> *Ask:* The angels are willing to help with anything we ask for. It doesn't matter how insignificant you may feel your request is or how hugely impossible the task appears to you. The angels are here to help us and provide us with their guidance, as long as it is for our highest good. For many, "for our highest good" is a difficult concept to understand, so I'll address that in a moment.

> *Thank*: Lastly, we all like to be thanked for our good deeds. It shows gratitude, and the more we feel appreciated, the more we want to help. The angels are no different on that score. They appreciate when we thank them for their love and support. It shows them that we are sincere in our asking and are grateful for their help. The more we thank our angels, the more they enjoy helping us, because they delight in seeing our appreciation for their work. So thank your angels, and thank them often. Then begin to notice how much more frequently you see signs that the angels are near.

Now back to the meaning of "for our highest good." Sometimes there are lessons we need to learn through difficult or uncomfortable situations. The help and guidance we receive from our angels may not necessarily be what we were expecting or hoping for. For example, you may be asking that a particular situation be taken away from your experience because it is causing you emotional pain or upset. Yet, it might be that this particular situation is present in your life to provide you with an opportunity to grow. Even though you may not see it at the time, that growth opportunity is for "your highest good," and the angels know this. Therefore, the angels may provide you guidance or situations that, at the time, don't appear to be taking the situation away, but are, indeed, for your highest good, allowing for a growth opportunity.

I recall such an experience where I was very upset with an outcome until I realized the higher-good growth opportunity. I had a boss, an assistant director in my department, who became ill and needed to be out of the office for an extended amount of time. During her leave, I kept her work up to date while doing my own. There came a time when she decided it best not to return, and her position became available. Since I had been doing her work for more than six months, I applied for the job. Another administrator in the office had confided in me that the job was mine and this would be announced soon. Two days later, enough time for a little political play to take place, the position was announced, and to the surprise of many, especially me, it was handed over to someone who had, months prior, left the office, but had now decided to come back. I was devastated. I didn't understand it. What had happened within those two days? Eventually, though, I understood. Six months later, I was promoted within my department to a position that greatly expanded my knowledge base in the field I was in. A year later, I was recruited by another organization, because of my vast experience in all phases of my field, to head a department as a director reporting to the president of the organization. If I had gotten that other position, I would not have had the opportunity to increase my knowledge and advance as I did. The angels had a plan in place. They did come to my aid, not originally as I had expected, but most definitely for my highest good.

Often, as time goes by, you can look back and acknowledge the lessons learned and growth experienced from your life situations, but the angels already know your path. So don't be discouraged if you don't get the answers or the situations presented that you think are in your best interest. You must have faith in the angels and believe that they do work for your highest good. Keep in mind also that there are times when lessons are karmic and not always so easy to grasp. Highest good in these cases can be disguised and even not realized at all. Faith is what the angels want us to have—faith that they are here with us, are always looking out for our best interest, and are always working on behalf of our highest good.

You may call upon the angels in any way you feel comfortable. You can call to them out loud, asking the angels to come to you and then asking for their help with your situation. Or you can request their help by just thinking those same thoughts to yourself. Silently or out loud, it doesn't matter. Nor does it matter whether or not you know what angel to call for your particular situation. You don't need to know that Archangel Raphael is the angel in charge of healing, or that Archangel Michael is our mighty protector, or that Archangel Haniel is the angel of love. All you really need to know in order to receive help is that you must invite the angels into your life and then ask them for help. If you call generically upon the angels, the right angel will come to you. But if you want to maximize the angelic connection and develop a mutual relationship with the angels, you will want to know whom to call for what situation and how to invoke that angel.

Here is a basic invocation for you to practice. But remember, there is no right or wrong way to speak with your angels. It is all about intention. In this basic invocation exercise, you are going to call to your primary guardian angel and ask for help in recognizing his or her presence now and in the future. Read through the basic invocation below before trying it, and then practice by invoking your primary guardian angel by name. Keep practicing until you have a sense of how your guardian is making him- or herself known to you. The process may take time, but be patient with yourself. Have compassion for yourself. Practicing and taking notes will help.

Exercise 1
Basic Invocation

❖ Sit in a comfortable position with straight back and feet flat on the floor if possible. Place your hands resting, palms up, on your lap.

❖ Begin by taking three slow, deep breaths, releasing any tension you feel as you exhale.

❖ When you are ready, close your eyes but continue to focus on your breathing. Inhale relaxation and exhale tension until you feel completely relaxed.

❖ When you are relaxed, begin to breathe normally and clear your mind by letting go of all thoughts, much like you do before you fall off to sleep. If thoughts pop into your mind, don't get upset or frustrated; just acknowledge them and bring your focus back to your breath. This happens often even to experienced meditators, so be kind to yourself and do the best you can, especially when first learning.

(The above section is the basic opening protocol for all the exercises contained in this book. You will also find it outlined in Chapter 4.)

As you continue to breathe normally, say, either out loud or to yourself, the name of your primary guardian angel. Say the name three times and then state your request. Follow your request by saying, "Sealed by your love and light, love and light, love and light." This shows the angels that your intention is sincere and pure. (An example would be "Gabriel, Gabriel, Gabriel, please give me a sign so I may recognize when you are near, sealed by your love and light, love and light, love and light.")

Once you have stated your request, you will need to notice any thoughts that come to your mind, any sensations you might feel in your body, any colors, shapes, numbers, or pictures that enter your mind's eye (this is your third-eye chakra area, your "inner eye" located between your physical eyes), or any sounds you might hear with your "inner ears" (this sounds similar to what you "hear" when you read silently to yourself). When you are ready, you will end with the following closing protocol (outlined again in Chapter 4).

- ❖ Thank your angel (this shows gratitude).
- ❖ Slowly open your eyes, focus on a few different objects around you, and wiggle your fingers and toes (this brings your attention to the present moment).
- ❖ If possible, drink a glass of water (this will ensure you are back and grounded).
- ❖ Write down what you noticed during your angelic connection.

Practice this exercise several times with your guardian angel, and each time, notice if you are receiving in the same way, such as the same sensations, colors, or sounds. If so, this will most likely be how your guardian angel connects with you. For example, if you feel a cool breeze on your left knee and you notice this every time you invoke your guardian angel, you can be certain that this is the way your angel is letting you know he or she is with you.

When you first begin practicing, the connection may happen immediately, or it may take several minutes, or you may not "get" anything at all. If you are unable to recognize a sign from your angel, don't get discouraged; just keep practicing, and eventually, it will come. Remember, the angels *want* to communicate with you, and they will continue to try their best to help you recognize their presence. In the beginning, try spending at least ten minutes on this exercise.

If you have made a connection with your guardian angel, it's now time to practice this same exercise with each of the remaining Sacred Seven angels. Notice the difference, if any, between your connection responses with each of the angels. Make sure to note them down in your journal. Some people may receive the same signal (such as a cool breeze, tingling sensations, colors, or sounds) every time they invoke an angel and may wonder which angel is with them. In this case, once you feel the breeze, just ask "Which angel is here?" and the first name coming into your mind is the angel who is with you. This is how I sense the angels. I am in a constant state of allowing the angels into my life, so when my hands become tingly for no apparent reason, I know immediately that the angels are with me. I silently, or sometimes not so silently, ask "Who is here?" and the first name that pops into my head is the angel I know is with me. If I don't receive a clear message, then I ask again. There is no harm in asking as many times as needed. When I do receive my answer, I thank the angel by name to acknowledge his or her presence, and then I might simply tell the angel I'm glad he or she is with me and go about my business. If something is weighing heavily on my mind, I'll talk as if I was talking to a close friend and receive inspiration regarding my concern.

chapter 4

see, hear, feel, know your angels are near

Angelic guidance is always gentle, loving, positive, and inspiring. How we receive our guidance is totally individualized. One person may "see," while another may "hear" or "feel," and then there are those who just "know." The angels communicate in ways that make us most likely to recognize their presence and understand their messages. Here, you are going to discover which way, or ways, work best for you. You will learn four methods of receiving messages from your angels. The French word *clair* translates to English meaning "clear," so the four methods you will learn about relate to clear seeing, clear hearing, clear feeling, and clear knowing.

Clairvoyance refers to seeing your messages, or "clear seeing." This is when the angels are sending you messages through your outer vision, inner sight through the third eye (often referred to as the mind's eye), or through your dreams. Keeping in mind that angel messages are often repetitive, some examples of clairvoyance include seeing colors, objects, words, or numbers repeatedly over a fairly short period of time. You may notice number sequences on license plates or digital numbers on clocks, or you may see through your mind's eye images, colors, shapes, objects, or even a scene playing out like a short movie in your mind. Contrary to popular belief, clairvoyance is not only seeing apparitions. Visual sequences, inner sight, and messages through dreams are actually more typical ways of receiving clairvoyant messages.

Clairaudience refers to hearing our messages. Since *audial* relates to the sense of hearing, you can easily remember that clairaudience refers to "clear hearing." This is when the angels are sending you words or sounds through the sense of hearing, either audibly or silently, which is similar to how you hear yourself when you are reading silently. Some examples of clairaudient messages are hearing your name being called when no one is calling you; hearing celestial music in your "inner ear"; overhearing a conversation or seeing a TV show with dialog that seems to be giving you the answers to the questions you've been asking; hearing the same song on the radio over and over again, either providing you with a message you understand or one that you come to understand within time; or having the lyrics of a song stuck in your head with the same reaction as the recurring song, one with immediate meaning or one that provides insight you didn't know you needed at the time. Angelic messages are often repetitive, so when you notice sounds being repeated, this may be your angels trying to get through to you clairaudiently.

Clairsentience, or "clear feeling," is when the angels are sending you messages through physical or emotional sensations. The sensations are felt somewhere on or in the body, such as having a gut feeling in the pit of your stomach or a sudden tingling in your hands. Other examples of clairsentient messages include feeling the sensation of a cool or warm breeze when the air is completely still; having butterflies in your stomach; getting goose bumps; or experiencing the emotional feeling of empathy. Even anxiety can be a message from our angels. Individuals who are clairsentient feel their messages.

Claircognizance, or "clear knowing," is the last of the four "clairs" being discussed here. Although it is generally least recognized, claircognizance is actually the most commonly experienced "clair." As a matter of fact, you most likely have experienced claircognizance and not even realized it. If I were to ask you if you have ever had an intuitive thought, I bet you would say yes. Experiencing intuition is not really the question as I'm sure most people have, even if referred to as instinct or perception. The real question here is whether or not you follow your intuition when you receive it. What if I told you that when you receive an intuitive thought, this is actually the angels "downloading" information into your crown chakra? Have you ever had a thought and wondered where it came from, or had a thought and said to yourself, "There's no way I could have known that"?

Often, our claircognizant experiences are beyond our current scope of knowledge, point of reference, or awareness. This is generally the first indicator that the angels are downloading messages to you and that you are not just concocting these thoughts, pulling them out of thin air. Unlike having a clairsentient "gut feeling" experience, the claircognizant experience comes through our cognitive mind as an actual "knowing." Those who are able to receive messages through automatic writing are experiencing the angels through claircognizance.

I have a story to share with you that pre-dates my awareness of many of the angels I have come to know and love. I tell this story because it shows that there are many different ways of noticing and confirming what you notice. Between 1994 and 1998, I studied polarity therapy, an energy-healing modality brought to the United States in the 1920s by Dr. Randolph Stone. Dr. Stone was an osteopath who studied Ayurvedic medicine in India in the 1920s. He blended eastern and western medicine and developed polarity therapy based on his definition of wireless anatomy and his work with the energy fields, currents, and movements in, through, and around our bodies. This energy work interested me and I began to study. I took formal classes at the Polarity Institute in Watertown, Massachusetts, and eventually became a registered polarity practitioner.

As a student, I remember the initial protocol being drummed into our heads: while cradling the heads of our student "clients," we would ask to be surrounded by light, release all negativity, place our egos behind us, create a fulcrum from the back of head at an angle down into the earth behind us to stabilize, and then ground with heaven and earth. It really worked (and still does). It placed me into a grounded, protected, neutral position where I became a conduit for healing energy.

As time went on, and I read and studied, I learned that Archangel Raphael is the angel of healing. I began to add him to my opening protocol, asking Raphael to be with me during the healings, always for the clients' highest good. During the first several sessions where I called upon Raphael, I noticed nothing different. But then one day, as soon as I called to him, I felt a distinct sensation running up and down the center of my back. At first, I paid little attention to it, but after a while, I noticed that every time I called Raphael's name, I got the same feather-like, tickling sensation up and down the center of my back. We now know I was having a clairsentient experience, although I didn't know it at the time. But I was intrigued. I thought, *Could this be Archangel Raphael letting me know he is with me?* I needed to know, so I began testing Raphael in a very playful way. Everywhere I went, I would call to Raphael. In the grocery store, standing in line: "Raphael, please come to me" I would say silently, and the tickling came. Driving my car: "Raphael, please come to me," I'd say out loud, and the same sensation came. "Raphael, Raphael, Raphael"—anytime I called to him, I would get that same feather-like, tickling sensation. It wasn't long before I began to believe that this is in fact Raphael's way of letting me know he is with me. Of course I continue to call to him during my healing sessions, but now I call him anytime I need healing for me or others, whether I'm doing a session or not. I know Archangel Raphael is always near.

I tell this story because I want you to know that not only do the angels come to us in ways that are easiest for us to notice them, but they are also persistent in their attempt to help us know they are near. Don't discount any sign you may get, no matter how small or insignificant you might think it is. Know that most initial connections come as small signs. Be aware; test the angels for reassurance, as I did. The angels don't mind, and they don't get annoyed; they love it when you start to recognize their signs. Remember that some people will be more adept at receiving visual signs through clairvoyance, others will hear their messages through clairaudience, still others will learn to recognize their feelings as a clairsentient message, and others will understand that their sense of knowing is the angels communicating with them claircognizantly. It takes time to develop relationships with the angels, so give yourself the time to practice noticing, and above all, have fun. Have fun playing with the angels, as I did when I kept calling to Raphael to come to me at all different times and places. The angels do have a sense of humor and will connect with you in fun and loving ways.

So now that you know a little about the four "clairs," do you have any idea what you might gravitate toward? Let's try some exercises to help you determine which one you best relate to. You may connect to one method strongly and not to the others, or you may be comfortable with more than one way of communicating with your angels. It's suggested that you read through the exercises in this section first before trying them. When you start to practice and complete an exercise, jot down your initial responses. This will help you down the road to determine what exercises were easiest for you and where, if at all, repetition is noted. After you have completed all exercises in this section, there is a chart to help you assess the ease or difficulty of receiving messages from each of the four "clairs." It will be beneficial for you to keep your notes in the journal provided at the back of the book so all your experiences are recorded in one place.

As you work through the exercises, try not to become discouraged. You may need to do each of the exercises several times before you begin to notice anything. It's important to learn to trust what you get and not let your ego get in the way by placing doubts in your mind. As you begin your exercises and are taking those relaxing breaths and clearing your mind of thought, try to imagine placing your ego (the thoughts of your conscious mind) temporarily "behind you." You may need to practice this by sending it back every time thoughts reenter your mind, but that's okay. Typical beginner-thoughts an ego will try to impose on you are "I'm not doing this right" or "I'm making this up" or "I should be doing something else (this or that)." Just take a moment to send the ego back behind you every time a thought disrupts your process. As time goes on, you'll need to do this less and less and eventually will only need to do it in the beginning. But for now, send the ego away as much as you need to. When you are done connecting with your angels and after you have thanked them, ask the ego to come back; it inevitably always will.

While mentioning the ego, what comes to mind is the difficulty many have with self-judgment. This is an important story about not judging yourself through this process. Many years ago, before my Polarity experience with Raphael, I began learning about the spirit world through a friend who was clairaudient. I wanted more than anything to "hear" like she did. Try as I might, ask as I did, begging and pleading to hear, no voices were giving me messages. I was frustrated and very down on myself. I wondered what was I doing wrong, why couldn't I hear like my friend; I actually thought that I must not be worthy of such a privilege. Of course, at the time, I didn't know there was more to being clairaudient than hearing with my outside ears. As time went on, I began to notice that when I closed my eyes at night to go to sleep, I saw colors. I noticed the colors coming in and fading out in all different shapes and color intensities. I thought everyone saw this when they closed their eyes, so even though I was noticing, I wasn't *aware* of what I was noticing. As time went on, when I looked up at my ceiling at night before going off to sleep, I would see sparkly lights of different colors, but especially silver and gold, like a night sky full of stars. Other times, I would be driving, and all of a sudden, I would hear music, like a choir of beautiful angelic voices, in one ear or the other. I thought I was just imagining it (my ego at work). Many years later, while taking an angel class with my dear mentor Emmanuelle Pries, I mentioned the night sparkles, and she enlightened me. "These are angels," she said. I told her about the other encounters, "Angels, angels," she said. Ever since then, when I see the colors or sparkles or hear the music, I smile and say "Thank you" to the angels for the gift of awareness, of being able to notice their presence and accept that as my truth. You see, it took me a long time to learn that I receive messages differently than my friend. So I pass on to you the gift of patience in finding, and the knowledge of accepting, that your truth in angels will come in time and in accordance with your highest good. Never compare your spiritual growth to that of others. Each soul is on its own path.

Following are exercises to help develop your "clairs." When you first start to practice, it is best to call upon your birth guardian angel, as this is the angel with the strongest vibrational connection to you. But you may, of course, practice with each of the seven angels you've just learned about, all at your own pace. In the beginning of each exercise, you will do the opening protocol, and you will end each exercise with the closing protocol. Take your time and enjoy the process.

You will begin by working toward receiving messages clairvoyantly.

Opening Protocol

- ❖ Sit in a comfortable position with your hands resting, palms up, on your thighs.
- ❖ Take three slow, deep breaths, releasing any tension as you exhale.

❖ When ready, close your eyes and continue to breathe; inhale relaxation, exhale tension.
❖ When relaxed, begin to breathe normally and clear your mind of all thoughts.

Closing Protocol

❖ Thank your angel.
❖ Slowly open your eyes, focus on a few different objects around you.
❖ Wiggle your fingers and toes.
❖ Drink a glass of water.
❖ Write down what you noticed during your angelic connection.

Exercise 2
Clairvoyance (a)

For this exercise, you will invoke your primary guardian or any of the seven birth guardians that you are drawn to. You will ask that angel to help you receive a message clairvoyantly. You will practice clairvoyance (clear seeing) by sharpening your imagination and internal sight.

❖ Begin with the opening protocol.
❖ Imagine you are holding down in front of you three helium balloons, each balloon being a different color.
❖ Keeping your head still, bring your closed eyes down to look at the balloons.
❖ Let one of the balloons go, and taking your time, watch (by raising your closed eyes but not moving your head) as it slowly floats up into the blue sky, up, up, floating past the white clouds, up higher and higher, until it disappears.

❖ Lower your closed eyes and gaze at the remaining two colored balloons; then release one, following as it floats up into the sky higher and higher until it disappears.

❖ Do the same with the third colored balloon, watching until you can no longer see it.

❖ Once all balloons are out of sight, with eyes remaining closed, call upon your angel to be with you and ask to be given a clairvoyant message, one that you need right now.

❖ Take your time and notice any images, symbols, or colors coming into your mind's eye.

❖ Finish with the closing protocol.

Exercise 3
Clairvoyance (b)

Another exercise to strengthen clairvoyance is practicing "soft eyes."

❖ Begin with the opening protocol.

❖ After your mind is clear of all thoughts, take a few moments to relax the muscles in your face by tightening and then releasing your facial muscles; next, tighten and relax your forehead, your eyes, your jaw, and your chin.

❖ With your relaxed eyes open, begin to focus on an object in the near distance.

❖ Stare at the object, holding it as your focal point until your eyes begin to tire (about one to two minutes).

❖ Allow your eyelids to gently begin to close until they are softly closed (so that the eyelids are closed but barely meet), and hold in this position for a minute or two.

❖ Keeping your closed eyes soft, ask your angels to give you a clairvoyant message, one that you need now.

❖ Notice any flashing colors, images, words, or numbers.

❖ Finish with the closing protocol.

Exercise 4
Clairaudience (a)

For this exercise, you will invoke your primary or any birth guardian that you are drawn to and ask that angel to help you receive a message clairaudiently. Here you will practice clairaudience (clear hearing) by sharpening your hearing of external sounds.

❖ Begin with the opening protocol.
❖ As you sit quietly, breathing comfortably, tune in to the sounds around you.
❖ Notice those sounds that appear to be close.
❖ Now notice sounds that seem to be farther away.
❖ Next, notice any sounds that are far off in the distance.
❖ Make sure you continue to breathe comfortably, and when you are ready, call to your angel asking to be given a clairaudient message.
❖ Notice any sounds or words coming to you through your inner ears.
❖ Finish with the closing protocol.

Exercise 5
Clairaudience (b)

You may also practice clairaudience by listening to music. For best results, choose music from the Baroque, Renaissance, or Classical periods. You will have this music playing softly throughout the exercise.

❖ Begin with the opening protocol.
❖ Remain relaxed and breathe normally as you listen to the music in the background.
❖ Ask your angel to help you "hear" a message clairaudiently through the music.

❖ Notice any messages coming through to your inner ears.

❖ Finish with the closing protocol.

Exercise 6
Clairsentience (a)

For this exercise, you will invoke any of the angels that you are drawn to and ask that angel to help you receive a message clairsentiently. Practice clairsentience (clear feeling) by tuning into and recognizing physical or emotional sensations in or around your body.

❖ Begin with the opening protocol.

❖ As you sit quietly, begin the process of tightening and then releasing parts of your body, beginning with your toes and working upward. Tighten and release your feet, calves, thighs, buttocks, lower abdomen, middle section, chest, arms, hands, shoulders, neck, face, and head.

❖ Next, place your hands over your heart area and invoke your angel, asking to be given a clairsentient message.

❖ Notice any physical or emotional sensation, such as tingly feelings in your fingers, toes, or anywhere on your body, or brushes of warm or cool breezes. Do you feel happy and want to laugh, or are you suddenly sad and feel as though you want to cry? Are you becoming anxious sitting there, or is there such a feeling of peace that you wish you could stay here in this moment forever? Whatever you are feeling, know that the angels are giving you a message and you are receiving your message clairsentiently.

❖ Finish with the closing protocol.

Exercise 7
Clairsentience (b)

This Clairsentient exercise is done with a partner. Have your friend bring you a photograph of a person whom you do not know but your friend does. Sit opposite your friend.

- ❖ Begin with the opening protocol.
- ❖ When your mind is clear of all thoughts, open your eyes.
- ❖ Gaze at the photo your friend is showing you and ask the angels to give you a clairsentient message about the person in the photo.
- ❖ Notice what you feel. Does the photograph make you feel happy or sad? Do you have a positive or negative gut feeling? Do these feelings give you a glimpse of the person in the photo?
- ❖ Describe to your friend some of the characteristics of the person based on what you feel and ask your friend for feedback. Does your friend confirm your feelings? You may want to switch roles and see if your partner can pick up clairsentiently on your photo.
- ❖ Finish with the closing protocol.

Exercise 8
Clairsentience (c)

Similar to the previous exercise, you will do this with a friend. Here you will practice using psychometry (through contact). Have your friend give you an inanimate object, such as a piece of jewelry worn by someone you don't know.

- ❖ Begin with the opening protocol.
- ❖ Holding the object given to you by your friend, ask the angels to give you a clairsentient message about the owner of the object.

❖ Notice what you feel and describe to your friend some of the characteristics of the owner of the object based on what you feel. Do you feel the owner is a happy person? Old or young? Alive or deceased? What might they do or have done as a profession? What are your gut feelings about this person? Does your friend agree?

❖ Finish with the closing protocol.

Exercise 9
Claircognizance (a)

Here you will practice claircognizance (clear knowing) by working with automatic writing. Do this exercise sitting at a table, and have a sheet of blank paper and a pen or pencil in front of you. Following the opening protocol, you may do this exercise with your eyes open or closed, but at first it is best to keep your eyes closed. It is also important to keep your mind clear of thought and allow the flow of information to be downloaded into your mind freely. Do not censor, correct, or judge. This exercise may take more practice.

❖ Begin with the opening protocol.

❖ When you are ready, pick up your pencil and call upon your angel to be with you. Ask that a claircognizant message be sent down through your crown chakra (located at the top of your head), into your writing arm, down to your hand, and into the pencil you are holding.

❖ Then imagine your crown chakra is open and there is an energetic funnel of light extending out from it. See your angel pouring a message through the light funnel down through and into your hand.

❖ Keeping your mind clear of all your thoughts, allow your hand to move, writing anything that comes into your mind. Take your time, and do not filter what or how you are writing.

❖ Finish with the closing protocol.

If you have trouble allowing the thoughts to move into your writing hand, you may want to practice the following exercise with the focus on your crown chakra.

Exercise 10
Claircognizance (b)

❖ Begin with the opening protocol.
❖ Bring your focus to your crown chakra.
❖ Imagine a small violet ball resting lightly on your crown.
❖ Now imagine this violet ball getting larger, expanding upward and outward, forming a cone or a funnel.
❖ Continue to extend this funnel from your crown up and out as much as is comfortable.
❖ Relax your face, your jaw, neck, and shoulders and continue breathing normally.
❖ When you are ready, ask your angel to give you a claircognizant message and pass it down through the funnel into your mind.
❖ When a thought comes into your mind, know this is your message being downloaded by the angels.
❖ When you are ready, retract the funnel into the small violet ball, and then release the ball.
❖ Finish with the closing protocol.

Now that you have practiced each of the exercises, possibly several times, go back to your notes and determine which exercise seemed easiest and most comfortable for you. Prioritize your experiences with the "clairs" by numbering them zero to four based on the ease or difficulty in receiving messages with four being easiest down to zero of not able to receive messages at all. You may want to go over each of the exercises again for this assessment.

4 = Easiest; 3 = fairly easy; 2 = difficult but received; 1 = difficult but not sure if received; 0 = did not receive any messages

Mark your score here:

- ❖ _____: Clairvoyant (clear seeing; exercise 2)
- ❖ _____: Clairvoyant (clear seeing; exercise 3)
  Clairvoyant Total:_____

- ❖ _____: Clairaudient (clear hearing; exercise 4)
- ❖ _____: Clairaudient (clear hearing; exercise 5)
  Clairaudient Total:_____

- ❖ _____: Clairsentient (clear feeling; exercise 6)
- ❖ _____: Clairsentient (clear feeling; exercises 7 or 8)
  Clairsentient Total:_____

- ❖ _____: Claircognizant (clear knowing; exercise 9)
- ❖ _____: Claircognizant (clear knowing; exercise 10)
  Claircognizant Total:_____

Often, especially when first learning, there is one "clair" that is easiest to work with. Practice the exercises again, beginning with the "clair" you scored the highest on. The highest may not be eight, but whatever number it is, begin there. If you scored a zero on all four of the "clairs," repeat all the exercises, or the ones that you are most comfortable with and see what you notice. If after practicing again, you still have trouble noticing a sound, sight, sensation, or knowing, it may be that your ego is interfering with the process and you are overthinking it. Very often, it is just a matter of allowing yourself to relax while doing the exercises and not self-doubting or judging. With practice, you will be able to receive your messages, but if you are having trouble, take a break from practicing. Continue reading, and when you are ready, return to practicing. Know that it's not unusual for there to be blocks when you first begin to work with the angels. Remember the story about me trying to receive messages like my clairaudient friend? If it doesn't come right away, don't be discouraged. The angels are with you always, but it may take a little time for your vibration to rise high enough for you to be able to perceive their messages. Meditating with Gabriel will help (see chapter 9 for meditations).

Once you have determined which "clair" is the easiest method for receiving messages and you've practiced connecting with your primary guardian, it's time to begin working with the other Sacred Seven angels. To do this, think of a question you want to ask, and invoke the angel best suited to give you the answer or guidance (see chapter 2). With your easiest "clair" method in mind, ask that angel to give you your message in that way, such as clairaudiently or clairsentiently. If all methods in your assessment chart are marked at the same level (such as all threes or all twos), ask the angel to give you the message in the easiest way for you to recognize. The angel will know what to do, and all you need to do is leave your ego behind and trust what you get. When you first start, it's helpful to select questions that are more general in nature rather than predictive. This is especially important during the time you are first developing your relationships with the angels. As you become more experienced at keeping your ego in check and your confidence and trust in the angels grows, you'll have no limit to the questions you can ask. But for now, keep it general, and to give you an idea, here are a few examples.

1. What do I need to do to increase my energy level (or health)? (Ask Raphael.)

2. What do I need to do to bring harmony and balance into my life? (Ask Cassiel.)
3. Please help me recognize the true abundances in my life. (Ask Zadkiel.)
4. How do I increase my feelings of self-confidence (or self-worth)? (Ask Camael.)

Once you have called upon your angel and stated your request for guidance, be still and patient, and notice. Notice anything that comes to you, whether it's one message—a single thought, feeling, picture, or sound—or several messages, one after another. Don't dismiss anything that comes to you, even if you don't understand what it means at first. Often, the meaning becomes clear over time. As you practice, your messages will become easier to recognize and their meanings will become clearer.

Unless you receive your messages through claircognizance (clear knowing), you will also need to develop associations for some of the symbols, sounds, or sensations you receive. For example, if you receive a flash of the color red in your mind's eye through clairvoyance, you will need to associate that flash with words that represent the color red to you, personally. One person might associate the red flash with driving and a red light. That association might be a message from the angels to stop what you're doing and look at the situation from all directions. Another person might associate the color red with power and take the flash to mean "Wear red at the job interview next week." Still another, who yearns for a sense of stability in life, may find the symbolism to mean "strengthen your foundation"—the root chakra, which is associated with the color red. Everyone is an individual, and a symbol or sign might mean one thing to one person and mean something totally different to another. The angels work to bring you messages through avenues that you personally will recognize and find meaning in. But how do you remember all the associations, especially in the beginning? Well, let's go back to the red flash. If you receive that color clairvoyantly and don't understand the association, you'll need to ask for clarity. The process will be the same: ask your angel for clarity on the message you just received, and then wait to see if you get a clarifying message or symbol. Relating to the examples above, does your clarifying message bring you a vision or flash of a car, meaning stop, a desk, meaning interview, or a house, meaning your foundation? It's a little like being a detective, figuring out the meaning of the leads you get from your angels. But once you start to get it, all begins to flow. In the beginning, you may need to ask for clarity several times for any one association. There's nothing wrong with that; ask until you understand.

From this point, you may want to jot down each association under the "My Personal Angel Dictionary" section provided at the back of the book. Do this for all the pictures, sounds, or feelings you receive as you practice receiving messages. This will become your angel dictionary - a personal reference to the specific angel language you share with the angels. You will always be able to refer back to it when you need more clarity on the symbolism of a message. Eventually, your messages will become clear as you become more in tune with the way you personally connect with the angels. But especially when you are first starting out, your personalized angel dictionary is an invaluable and handy tool.

chapter 5

meet the zodiac angels

If you recall from chapter 2, where you were introduced to your birth guardian angel, everyone has at least two guardians. On the day you were born, not only did you receive a birth guardian who remains with you throughout your life, but also, at the precise moment of your birth, with sun, moon, and planets aligned, another angel came to you and serves as your second primary guardian, your zodiac guardian angel. Your guardians watch over you and forever act as advisors, protectors, guides, and more. Like the Sacred Seven, the zodiac angels have very specific roles that help guide you in all aspects of your life. I first learned of these angels through the work of Angela McGerr, but unlike several of the birth guardians, whose names I knew, I had never heard of any of the zodiac angels (nor many of the nature angels you will learn about in the next chapter). This might be true for you as well. Although you may not be familiar with these angel names, try not to get stuck there, preventing you from receiving their love, guidance, and support. As I continued to work with the zodiac angels, it soon became clear that their guidance was gentle but firm, sending me in a direction that I had been trying to go in for a very long time. I was stuck for sure, and their support became an invaluable part of my life's journey. I hope you will also find this to be so, and to help you, I created a flow chart called "My Zodiac Angel Focus Wheel for Change." You'll find it at the end of this chapter. Use it for figuring out and working through any goals or life changes you want for yourself, especially if you're stuck or resistant, consciously or unconsciously, to the change you need or think you might need, in order to accomplish those goals. This method is one that helps you make gradual change for life's transformational events over the course of a year.

You can call upon any of the zodiac angels at any time for assistance, but the energy of these angels is strongest and most easily felt during their corresponding zodiac cycle. As with your birth guardian, you will want to develop a special relationship with your zodiac guardian. While the experience of receiving guidance from many different angels throughout your lifetime is commonly called having a guardian angel, these angels come and go, in and out of lives, according to the needs of the individuals at the time. So, for example, an angel might come to help a student who is studying for an exam, and then leave after the exam is over. Or an angel might come to help a person with their self-confidence during a job interview, but then leave when the interview is over. The two people in these examples may very well thank their "guardian angel" and angels definitely were on the job, but the difference between these angels and your two primary guardian angels is that your birth guardian and zodiac guardians never leave your side.

In the pages that follow, you will be introduced to the zodiac angels. One of them is your guardian. With each angel, included are two mini-meditations to help you connect and begin to develop a relationship as well as serve as examples of how you can begin to craft your own requests for guidance. Begin all mini-meditations with opening protocol found in Chapter 4, then invoke the zodiac angel.

CAPRICORN'S NADIEL
A Time for Self-Evaluation

If you were born between December 22 and January 19, under the sun sign Capricorn, your zodiac guardian angel is Nadiel. She is an angel who helps you evaluate your life, viewing your challenges as opportunities for growth and assisting you in overcoming those challenges as you travel the road toward change. Nadiel brings you peace and tranquility, eliminating feelings of being overwhelmed or tendencies to lack self-confidence. From this vantage point, you are better able to identify your true heart's desire.

Call upon Nadiel for help in finding your heart's desire through personal evaluation and for overcoming challenges that get in your way of happiness.

Exercise 11
Mini-Meditations with Nadiel

To Find Your True Desire

"Nadiel, Nadiel, Nadiel, please be with me now and help me to clarify my heart's desire and to embrace all personal change needed to bring this desire into my life."

Sit quietly for at least ten minutes, thank Nadiel, and then write down any thoughts that entered your mind. With this new information, you may begin to make changes in your life.

To Evaluate and Overcome Challenges

"Nadiel, Nadiel, Nadiel, please be with me now and help me to overcome and conquer the challenges that have been blocking my success and happiness; guide me toward my heart's desire." (Name your heart's desire, and be as specific as you can.)

Be still and allow yourself to receive your message from Nadiel. Thank Nadiel, then write down your thoughts.

AQUARIUS'S CAMBIEL
A Time to Prioritize Actions

If you were born between January 20 and February 18, under the sun sign Aquarius, your zodiac guardian angel is Cambiel. He is an angel of prioritizing action steps for transformation, and he encourages you to listen to and follow your intuition. Trusting your intuitive thoughts is the first step toward the process of change. If you haven't already determined what you want changed in your life, Cambiel can help. If while you are identifying your action step, it elicits feelings of being overwhelmed or confused, Cambiel can also help. If you have worked with Capricorn's angel Nadiel on identifying your challenges, Cambiel can further that effort by helping eliminate any ego self-talk that may be interfering with your process.

Call on Cambiel to give you a clear understanding of which steps to take first for achieving your goals and for help in trusting your intuition.

Exercise 12
Mini-Meditations with Cambiel

For Prioritizing Action

"Cambiel, Cambiel, Cambiel, please be with me now and help me prioritize the steps I need to take to achieve the transformation I seek in life."

Sit for at least ten minutes, thank Cambiel, and then write down any thoughts that entered your mind. With this new information, you may begin to make changes in your life.

For Accepting Your Intuition

"Cambiel, Cambiel, Cambiel, please be with me now and help me to have the confidence to truly believe what my inner self tells me and to accept the guidance of my intuition as it directs me toward self-transformation." (State your goals here, and be as specific as you can.)

Be still and allow your messages to come. Thank Cambiel, and then write down your thoughts.

PISCES'S BARAKIEL
A Time for Clarity

Barakiel is your guardian angel if you were born between February 19 and March 20, under the sign of Pisces. Barakiel (the only zodiac angel that rules two signs, Pisces and Scorpio) is an angel of clarity. It is with his help, through a process of discernment, that one can clearly see one's way toward emotional healing. This is not always an easy path, though. As you progress through your journey of transformation, you will need to review the relationships in your life. You will need to separate who or what has a positive effect on you from those people and things that do not. Barakiel helps you to evaluate these relationships while also protecting you from any emotional stresses you may experience during the process.

Call to Barakiel for help in clearly identifying the positive and negative influences in your life and for guidance on how to best eliminate the negative and embrace the positive.

Exercise 13
Mini-Meditations with Barakiel

For Receiving Clarity

"Barakiel, Barakiel, Barakiel, please be with me now and help me to clearly distinguish between what has a positive influence on my life and what negative influences are causing blocks to my success and happiness."

Sit quietly for at least ten minutes, thank Barakiel, and then write down any thoughts that entered your mind.

For Guidance to Make Changes

"Barakiel, Barakiel, Barakiel, please be with me now and guide me to make the necessary changes for eliminating the negative and moving forward toward the positive in my life. As I begin to heal, please be sensitive to the difficulty I may have in realizing and accepting the truth, and help me to have self-compassion during this process."

Be still and allow the energy of Barakiel to give you the messages that you need. Thank Barakiel. Then write down your thoughts. With this new information, you may now begin to weed out the negative influences in your life.

ARIES'S MACHIDIEL
A Time to Find Heart's Desire

Machidiel is your zodiac guardian angel if you were born between March 21 and April 19, under the sign of Aries. Machidiel is an angel that helps us to gather the courage to reexamine our life purpose and restructure our goals according to our true heart's desire. While working with Pisces's Barakiel, you learned to discern between relationships that serve or do not serve your best interest; working with Machidiel will help you discern between following your head and following your heart. If you have felt frustrated or unfulfilled by the path you have been following and are ready to find and follow the true desire of your own heart, Machidiel can help. Machidiel teaches that our life purpose can only truly be recognized through the opening of our hearts, and this takes love and compassion for self.

Call upon Machidiel for help finding your passion and opening your heart to true happiness.

Exercise 14
Mini-Meditations with Machidiel

For Help Discerning between Head and Heart

"Machidiel, Machidiel, Machidiel, please be with me now and help me know the difference between what my head tells me I *should* do and what my heart knows I *must* do to live a happy life."

Sit quietly for at least ten minutes, thank Machidiel, and then write down any thoughts that entered your mind.

For Help Finding Your Life Purpose

"Machidiel, Machidiel, Machidiel, please be with me now and guide me toward uncovering my heart's desire, which will lead me toward my life purpose and true fulfillment."

Be still and allow Machidiel's messages to come to you. Thank Machidiel, and then write down your thoughts. As you do, a new life purpose may begin to unfold.

TAURUS'S TUAL
A Time to Let Go

Tual is the guardian for those born between April 20 and May 20, under the sign of Taurus. He is the angel of self-confidence and self-appreciation. If you began working with Picses's Barakiel on identifying the people, places, and situations that no longer serve you, with Tual you will further that work by gaining the confidence to hold firmly to your convictions by letting go of what is weighing you down. Tual can help you move forward toward a positive future by eliminating old conditioning and replacing it with self-acceptance, self-appreciation, and self-love, all keys to happiness.

Call upon Tual for help in strengthening your sense of personal power and for letting go of all that is not serving the fulfillment of your hopes and dreams. Tual's focus is letting go.

Exercise 15
Mini-Meditations with Tual

For Strengthening Your Sense of Personal Power

"Tual, Tual, Tual, please be with me now and help me to see the goodness in my heart; give me the strength to keep grounded in my thoughts and the confidence to remain true to my personal convictions, as I prepare to take actions toward letting go of what holds me back from realizing my heart's desire."

Sit quietly for at least ten minutes, thank Tual, and then write down any thoughts that entered your mind.

For Letting Go

"Tual, Tual, Tual, please be with me now and help me to let go, releasing any and all negative attachments that hold me back from fulfilling my dreams. Also help me to easily recognize and immediately let go of, any of these attachments that attempt to reenter my life."

Be still and allow your messages to come. Thank Tual and write down your thoughts.

GEMINI'S AMBRIEL
A Time for Integration

Ambriel is the zodiac guardian angel of all those born between May 21 and June 20, under the sign of Gemini. Ambriel is an angel who helps you take care of yourself often, while attending to others. If you have ever found it difficult to balance your needs against the needs of others, leaving you with a lack of energy or a feeling of being overwhelmed, overextended, or taken advantage of, call to Ambriel for assistance. Ambriel can help you sort it all out, refocus, regain, and rebalance your energy levels so that you can better attend to your own personal needs. A strong, healthy personal constitution lends more to helping others than a depleted one.

Call upon Ambriel to help you create and integrate healthy boundaries between your own needs and those of others, and for being true to yourself. Ambriel's focus is Integration.

Exercise 16
Mini-Meditations with Ambriel

For Rebalancing Your Energy Levels

"Ambriel, Ambriel, Ambriel, please be with me now and help me bring my energy levels into balance and then integrate my newfound energy so that it remains part of my life."

Sit quietly for at least ten minutes, thank Ambriel, and then write down any thoughts that entered your mind.

For Remaining True to Self

"Ambriel, Ambriel, Ambriel, please be with me now and guide me toward being able to speak up and express my true feelings in a compassionate way, especially when I am unable to provide others the assistance needed due to my own needs."

Be still and allow Ambriel's messages to be received. Thank Ambriel, and then write down your thoughts.

CANCER'S MURIEL
A Time for Self-Reliance

If you were born between June 21 and July 22, under the sign of Cancer, Muriel is your zodiac guardian. Muriel is an angel of self-reliance and can assist you in expressing your inner voice and taking the most efficient action steps forward to accomplish your goals. She can also help you strengthen your sense of personal power and resolve any conflicts that may be holding you back from attaining a life of pure joy. In short, Muriel helps you to rely on you!

Call upon Muriel for removing blocks hindering your success and for help developing a sense of self-reliance.

Exercise 17
Mini-Meditations with Muriel

For Removing Blocks and Finding Happiness

"Muriel, Muriel, Muriel, please be with me now and remove any blocks preventing me from moving forward in my life. Please help me find the happiness I know I deserve."

Sit quietly for at least ten minutes, thank Muriel, and then write down any thoughts that entered your mind.

For Becoming Self-Reliant

"Muriel, Muriel, Muriel, please be with me now and provide me the strength to find my personal power so that I can build the self-confidence needed to become self-reliant."

Be still and allow the energy of Muriel to come to you. Thank Muriel, and then write down your thoughts.

LEO'S VERCHIEL
A Time for Leadership

Verchiel is the angel of Leo, and if you were born between July 23 and August 22, he is your zodiac guardian. Verchiel is an angel of creative leadership. He brings balance between power and leadership and can instill within you a humble yet sound confidence devoid of egotistical implications. This will enable to you to creatively inspire those you lead, without having fear, doubt, or second-guessing yourself, thus aiding and encouraging them to reach their fullest potential. This holds true for leading yourself to success as well. Through his guidance, Verchiel can help bring out these leadership qualities, guiding you to follow your intuition.

Call to Verchiel if it is your time to step into a leadership role.

Exercise 18
Mini-Meditations with Verchiel

For Humble Confidence

"Verchiel, Verchiel, Verchiel, please be with me now and help me to know that one of my greatest strengths is possessing a sense of humble confidence, allowing me to lead without ego, helping others find their path."

Sit quietly for at least ten minutes, thank Verchiel, and then write down any thoughts that entered your mind.

For Instilling Creative Leadership

"Verchiel, Verchiel, Verchiel, please be with me now and help me be creative in my leadership role; provide me with the insight and skills needed to lead responsibly, inspiring others to excel in their own right."

Be still and allow Verchiel's message to come to you. Thank Verchiel, and then write down your thoughts.

VIRGO'S HAMALIEL
A Time for Well-Being

Hamaliel is your zodiac guardian if you were born between August 23 and September 22, under the sign of Virgo. Hamaliel is an angel who guides you to take care of your health in order to maintain the energy levels needed for you to work through any situation that might arise. Like Pisces's Barakiel, Hamaliel encourages you to address the relationships in your life to determine what is beneficial and what is not. Hamaliel can help you clearly see if you are in a harmonious state of energy exchange, meaning that what you are giving out and what you are receiving are in balance. It is then that you are in a place of well-being and find that the abundances in your life are very clear.

Invite Hamaliel into your life when you need to balance your relationships and aspire to live a life of well-being and abundance.

Exercise 19
Mini-Meditations with Hamaliel

For Balancing Relationships

"Hamaliel, Hamaliel, Hamaliel, please be with me now to help me find balance between what I give and what I take; help me focus on those relationships that are mutually satisfying."

Sit quietly for at least ten minutes, thank Hamaliel, and then write down any thoughts that entered your mind.

For Attaining a Sense of Well-Being

"Hamaliel, Hamaliel, Hamaliel, please be with me now and help me find and maintain a healthy sense of well-being. With this newfound well-being, please allow me to clearly see and be grateful for the abundance in my life."

Be still and allow Hamaliel's messages to come to you. Thank Hamaliel, and then write down your thoughts.

LIBRA'S ZURIEL
A Time to Assimilate

If you were born between September 23 and October 22, under the sign Libra, Zuriel is your zodiac guardian. Zuriel is an angel of love and compassion and can be quite instrumental in gently yet firmly eliminating old patterns no longer serving your highest good. If you have placed unkind or unrealistic judgments upon yourself or have behavioral patterns you wish to change, Zuriel can help dissolve them and provide you with a blueprint for change. Once accepted, Zuriel can also help you assimilate these new patterns into your life.

Call upon Zuriel to help you eliminate old patterns and assimilate the new.

Exercise 20
Mini-Meditations with Zuriel

To Recognize and Eliminate Old Patterns

"Zuriel, Zuriel, Zuriel, please be with me now and help me recognize those patterns no longer useful to me; with love and compassion, help me eliminate any unkind or unrealistic self-judgments."

Sit quietly for at least ten minutes, thank Zuriel, and then write down any thoughts that entered your mind.

To Assimilate Change

"Zuriel, Zuriel, Zuriel, please be with me now and help me to assimilate my newfound healthy patterns and bring balance to my body, mind, and soul so that I may move forward in the way that is most beneficial for my highest good."

Be still and allow Zuriel's messages to come to you. Thank Zuriel, and then write down your thoughts.

SCORPIO'S BARAKIEL
A Time to Move Forward

If you were born between October 23 and November 21, under the sign of Scorpio, Barakiel is your zodiac guardian angel (also guardian to those born under Pisces). In Scorpio, Barakiel helps lessen risks by bringing all the pros and cons of any decision or project into clear view. He helps you evaluate your opportunities for success before you take the plunge. Barakiel's guidance is especially important for those who are considering a major life change, as well as those starting a new venture.

Call upon Barakiel when you have a decision to evaluate or if you need help moving forward with a decision already made.

Exercise 21
Mini-Meditations with Barakiel

To Evaluate the Pros and Cons of Change

"Barakiel, Barakiel, Barakiel, please be with me now and help me identify the pros and cons of starting something new in my life. Please help me to sort out the benefits from the drawbacks and to accept the truth of each."

Sit quietly for at least ten minutes, thank Barakiel, and then write down any thoughts that entered your mind.

To Move Forward with a New Undertaking

"Barakiel, Barakiel, Barakiel, please be with me now, guiding me forward in a positive way in relation to my new venture, and help me remain focused so that I recognize each new step, one at a time, that leads me closer to realizing my desired outcome."

Be still and allow Barakiel to bring you his messages. Thank Barakiel, and write down your thoughts.

SAGITTARIUS'S ADNACHIEL
A Time for Expansion

Adnachiel is your zodiac guardian angel if you were born between November 22 and December 21, under the sign of Sagittarius. Adnachiel is an angel of joy, abundance, and expansion. She helps you identify your new personal goals by looking to your past for what has given you joy and what has caused you disappointment. Once you have looked at where you have been, she can help eliminate the blocks that prevent your growth and help you expand and envision a new path to travel. Adnachiel is all about vision and expansion for the purposes of providing you joy and abundance. Note that joy creates a field of expansion, while disappointment creates a state of contraction.

Invoke Adnachiel when discerning between joy and disappointment or to illuminate your expanded vision.

Exercise 22
Mini-Meditations with Adnachiel

To Identify Joy Versus Disappointment

"Adnachiel, Adnachiel, Adnachiel, please be with me now and help me see the difference between what gives me joy and what causes me disappointment."

Sit quietly for at least ten minutes, thank Adnachiel, and then write down any thoughts that entered your mind.

For Expanding Vision

"Adnachiel, Adnachiel, Adnachiel, please be with me now and help me see those opportunities presented to me for expansion; guide me toward realizing the new goals I envision for myself."

Be still and allow Adnachiel's message to come to you. Thank Adnachiel, and then write down any thoughts that entered your mind.

Working Through a Year with the Zodiac Angels

By now, I'm sure you have gotten the idea of how to go about creating your requests to the zodiac angels. This holds true for all angels you are learning about. You don't need a whole long process to invite the angels into your life. However you choose to work with them will be right for you. To begin working with the zodiac angels, regardless of the time of year, it's best to start with your zodiac primary guardian. Develop a relationship with your angel in the same way you did your birth guardian, by practicing how to invoke and how to recognize when your angel is with you. Go back and practice the "clairs" with your zodiac angel to determine which way you best receive your messages. See if the signs and methods differ from the way your birth primary guardian connects with you. Sometimes different angels have their own signature way of communicating with you, and sometimes it's the same for all angels, which is the case with me, except for Raphael. Just remember, each person has his or her own way of communing with the angels, and there is no wrong way.

It would be ideal, but not necessary, to start your transformation process during Capricorn with Nadiel, where you will self-evaluate and begin the process of overcoming challenges. However, if the end of December or beginning of January is too far away from your starting point, you may begin during any sign with the focus of the angel governing that sign and work completely through the year. As you work with the angel affiliated with the zodiac sign you are currently in, always call your primary zodiac guardian to oversee the process. While your guardian angel has a specific focus and you will indeed work with that focus during that angel's sign, your guardian is always with you, ready to help in any way. If you are having trouble progressing in any areas of focus during the year, not only will the angel governing that sign be there to help you, but so will your zodiac guardian. You will find your guardian to be especially strong, bringing protection and strength and an extra boost of energy to help you through the process. Take the time to really get to know your zodiac guardian before you start working with other zodiac angels. When you are ready, use the following completed focus wheel chart as a sample and then try your own in Exercise 23. You will find two blank charts for additional use at the back of the book.

Before you begin, you will need to give some thought to your desired focus. This should be something you want to accomplish within the year; something that is reasonably within reach even if you have no idea how you will accomplish it. For example, asking for a new job that pays you a million dollars when currently you earn thirty thousand dollars a year is not realistic. However, requesting a new job that makes you happy and pays you more than you currently earn, is a very reasonable request. You will want to narrow your statement of desire down into one or two sentences and place it in the My Focus space provided in the center circle.

Starting with the month and zodiac sign you are currently in, go back to review the attributes of the governing angel and ask for guidance in relation to your focus. For instance, if you are starting in the beginning of May, you are in Taurus and working with Tual. He is the angel that helps you let go, so once you have your focus for the year written out, ask Tual to help you figure out what you need to let go of in order to realize your goal. But if you are starting in Libra, you might ask Zuriel what it is you need to assimilate into your life in order to move forward with your goals. Once you have started, continue clockwise around the zodiac wheel asking the corresponding angels for guidance with regard to your goal and work through the associated process. Note that in the sample wheel I begin work with **Zuriel** and then move on to Barakiel, Adnachiel, Nadiel, and so forth. Continue working with each zodiac angel for the whole month before moving on to the next. Do your mini-meditations or create your own meditations; have fun with it. If you are finding resistance in any one area, in addition to asking your zodiac primary guardian for additional help, you may also request support and guidance from your birth guardian. Your birth and zodiac guardians work very well together. When you have moved through the twelve signs, completing the year, evaluate your progress and celebrate your success. You might even want to choose a new goal for the following year.

SAMPLE: My Zodiac Angel Focus Wheel for Change

Month and Day - Beginning with Angel: *October 3rd - Zuriel*

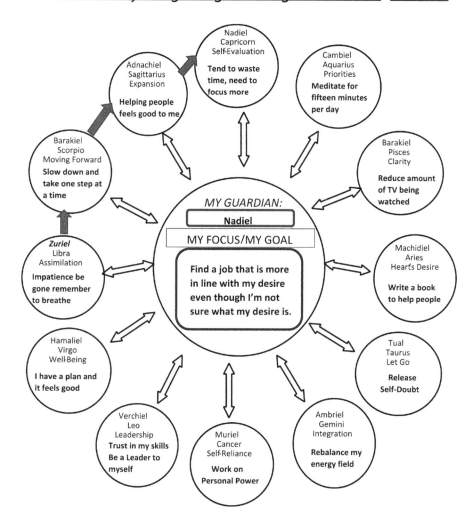

OUTCOME: I created and then began working this wheel in October. I gained the insight and discipline needed and eventually set a plan in motion that dedicated specific time to writing. This book is the result. Thank you, Angels!

Exercise 23
My Zodiac Focus Wheel for Change

Instructions:

❖ Insert in the heading the month and day you begin the wheel and the angel associated with that zodiac sign.

❖ In the large center circle write the name of your zodiac guardian angel.

❖ Determine your focus and write your statement in the center circle.

❖ Based on the zodiac sign you begin with, review the attributes of the governing angel.

❖ Ask for guidance in relation to the angel's attributes using the mini-meditation style; create your own as it relates to your focus.

❖ Continue clockwise around the zodiac wheel spending one month with each angel. First review the angel's attributes, then ask for guidance in relation to your focus.

❖ Proceed around the wheel until you have completed the entire twelve month cycle.

❖ At the end of your cycle, evaluate your progress and note the outcome of your work.

MY ZODIAC ANGEL FOCUS WHEEL FOR CHANGE

Month and Day/Beginning Angel:_____

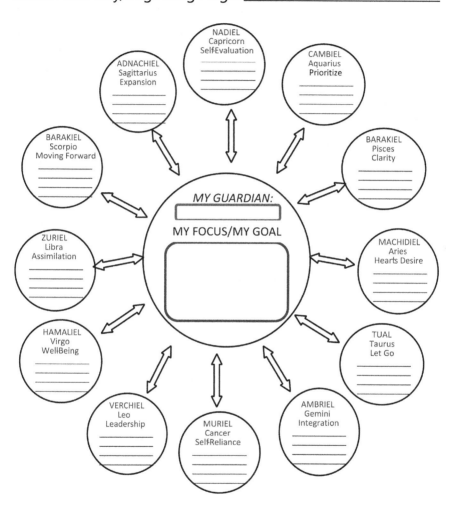

OUTCOME:

chapter 6

meet the nature angels

Ever since I was a little girl, I have loved nature. I grew up in the suburbs of Westchester County in New York during a time that predated computers, iPads and cell phones. As children, what we did in our neighborhood and in neighborhoods all around the country was spend a lot of time playing outside. My neighborhood included streets that saw little traffic and were surrounded by woods with streams that spawned pollywogs, paths to horse stables, apple orchards, and even an old, run-down, abandoned private school. Summer days were filled with kickball, tag, hide-and-seek, lying on the grass gazing up at the clouds, listening to the chirping birds, riding bicycles, and exploring uncharted territory. We didn't get called on a cell phone to come in for lunch or home for dinner, but when we heard the distinct sound of a mother's voice bellowing through the air, we all knew whose dinner was ready. If you're of the Baby Boomer age, you may know exactly what I'm talking about. If you're not, imagine a mother stepping out onto her front porch, cupping her hands around her lips, taking a real deep breath, and calling with all her might, *"Johnny and Baa-beeeee!"* Most of the time, Mrs. Loguercio only had to call once, but the message was loud and clear; it was time for Johnny and Bobby to go home.

Some of my favorite childhood memories are of exploring the woods with my neighborhood friends. I didn't realize then that I was being given a very precious gift, the gift of appreciation for nature's beauty, and in addition to that, being prepared to get to know the nature angels and all their secrets at a much later time in my life.

According to the Merriam-Webster dictionary, the word nature refers to "the physical world and everything in it that is not made by man" and "the natural forces that control what happens in the world." The nature angels are guardians of all that is living in our physical world; they govern all the forces of the elements responsible for movement, including the powerful energy that changes the seasons and causes rain, snow, fire, and winds. Nature angels oversee the amazing phenomena and command our respect and appreciation. They are happy when they see we are respectful, and they enjoy working by our side to help us understand, grow, and live in balance and harmony within nature. It's important to point out here that contrary to popular belief, nature angels are not fairies. Although fairies may have a strong relationship with nature, there are considerable differences between the two. Angels hold a higher vibrational frequency and always work for the highest good of all involved; and unlike fairies, angels will never be devious or play tricks on you—although I have found that some angels do have a sense of humor and will play with you, but always in a fun-loving way and never at your expense.

To connect with the nature angels, all you really need to do is to notice nature's beauty. There are four elements that make up that beauty in our physical world: earth, air, fire, and water. The elements of earth and air are overseen by Archangel Ariel, also known as nature's overseer and protector. Archangel Ariel oversees all that is associated with the earth, including how this element relates to us as human beings. The earth element governs the core foundation of life, our physicality, how we move about in this world. Do we walk our path, no matter what it is, in comfort or distress? The earth element is connected to the root chakra and to the color red. When this element is out of balance, the effect can present itself in several different ways. We may experience this imbalance physically, emotionally, or spiritually. A deficit may cause distress manifesting in tension headaches, anxiety-creating palpitations, or fear leaving you in a fright, flight, or frozen state. You may also experience feelings of insecurity, low self-esteem, or in extreme deficit, feelings of doom. On the other hand, if your earth element is out of balance due to excess, it may cause you to be unrealistically over-confident or impatient with people who don't "see it your way," or to be overly aggressive. You may also have a feeling of being different from others and may have trouble making and keeping friends. Ariel and the earth angels are happy to help and may be called upon for any situation having to do with an unbalanced foundation or root chakra.

You may be wondering, besides Ariel, who are the earth angels? I'm not talking about those people who are dear to you, who always come through when you need them, and whom you refer to as "angels" in your life. Nor am I speaking of those special people who humbly give their help and spread light wherever they go, and who are often called lightworkers. While both of these "angels" are very real and do walk the earth, making it a better place to live, I'm talking about the pure, high-vibrational frequency of angel energy here. Noticing these earth angels takes quieting your mind, slowing your breath, opening your heart, and allowing yourself to become aware. So, if you're outside, look up and notice the trees above you, or go to a window and look outside. If no trees are in your view, look at a photo or painting of trees. Although you may not know that Zuphlas is the guardian of trees, if you just stop a moment and allow yourself to become aware, noticing the expansion of branches, the beauty of the leaves and stability of the trunk, you can be assured that you are in the presence of earth angel, Zuphlas. If you look up at those expanded branches high above you, taking note of the green leaves softly contrasted against the blue sky, feeling a sense of strength from the firm foundation of the trunk, and are in awe, then Zuphlas has touched you in a way that is letting you know he is here. If you wish, Zuphlas can help you find ways to expand, to find your own beauty, and to live within a firm foundation of your own setting. Allow Zuphas to fill your heart with nature's wonders and strength. Notice trees in any of their forms, and Zuphlas, guardian of the trees, will let you know he is near.

As I was writing this book, I received a message from Zuphlas—but first, a prologue to the story. I drove the same way to work for ten years. Half my drive was down a street lined on both sides with glorious, strong, majestic-looking trees. Each morning as I drove to work, I would thank Zuphlas for sharing his beauty with me. I would notice the trees in all their seasonal dress—sometimes full with summer greenery, other times splashed in autumn colors, and then there was winter's bareness, showing such beauty in their core strength. It always put me into a good mood, which set up my day to be filled with gratefulness, joy, and love. My heart felt expanded each day when I reached this road. About a year prior to writing this chapter, I accepted a position at a different organization, and while driving to my new job, I noticed something that appeared odd. One particular road, also lined with trees on both sides, was bordered by an embankment of land that slanted upward approximately six feet before leveling off again. All of the trees whose roots were based in this embankment looked weak. Some trees were thin, some tall and straggly, and some were bent down so low toward the road that I thought at any moment a strong wind or rain could easily dislodge them and blow these trees away. I recall thinking how much I missed my previous route, where the trees stood tall, strong, and majestic, and how wonderfully peaceful, secure, and happy I had felt each day driving to work. Now all the trees on my route looked deficient in strength, and scrawny. Not one did I notice stood tall; not one huge, majestic tree did I see. So I asked Zuphlas one day why many of the trees on my current route were so weak. The message I received made perfect sense, and I knew it was meant to be shared with you. Zuphlas told me that the importance, that day, of noticing the earth beneath these straggly-looking trees was a lesson of foundation. In life, a strong foundation is vital to the development and growth of a healthy body, mind, and soul; a foundation lacking stability cannot support such growth. While not everyone is fortunate enough to begin life supported by a sturdy foundation, if someone's inner core is strong, within time, that person can find ways to repair and even completely rebuild his or her foundation to stand strong and be capable of withstanding life's storms. Then Zuphlas guided my eyes through the trail to this one spot where, among all the straggly trees, stood a huge tree with its roots planted firmly into that same embankment, from which it rose tall, solid, and very regal-looking. I stared for a moment before chuckling as I acknowledged to Zuphlas, that yes, I had gotten his point. Nature has so much to teach us, if only we stop and take notice.

Another angel that guards the earth and has so much to teach us is Sachluph, guardian angel of the plants. Sachluph protects all nature's wonders, bringing forth the opportunity for us to experience the richness and beauty, the calmness in presence, and the peacefulness of mind and heart that plants offer. Sachluph helps us to slow our movement down enough to notice, through our senses of sight, smell, sound, and touch, the gifts plants bestow. Have you ever stood in awe as you noticed the beautiful colors caressing a bed of flowers? You may see the beauty through your eyes, but the next time, try closing your eyes and feeling that beauty by taking it right into your heart. Through this effort, Sachluph will help to bring you a sense of calmness. Have you ever walked through a garden and smelled a sweet fragrance wafting through the air as you pass by? The next time, why don't you stop a moment and consciously inhale that fragrance, allowing the sweet smell of nature to surround and fill you? In doing so, you invite Sachluph to help to bring a sense of peace to your day. Have you ever heard the sound leaves make as they are gently being caressed by the wind? The sound can be almost trancelike. Take notice the next time you are near a tree when the wind begins to blow. Stand with your eyes closed and listen to the sound the leaves make as they dance through the air. Sachluph will surely help bring a sense of relaxation to you if you let her. However, if you think you're too busy to take time to notice, that too Sachluph can help with; just ask her to help you find time to spend with plants. It doesn't matter if you're surrounded by trees in a forest, by flowers or vegetables in a garden, or by potted plants on the windowsill of a city apartment; Sachluph can help you absorb the beauty plants have to offer and, in return, bring a sense of peace and tranquility into your life.

The medicinal properties of plants and how they can help us are Aratron's specialties, as he is guardian of nature's secrets. These secrets are the ones shamans are attuned to and have used for ages. The ancient mysteries of plants are guarded and protected from misuse by Aratron, but if you show intent to use this wisdom for the highest good of all, including Mother Earth, Aratron will share it with you. We live in a society of advanced allopathic medical practices, so it's important that Aratron guide you to use the ancient healing secrets in balance and harmony with modern medicine. He can help you evaluate the pros and cons in a discerning way. My experience in herbal remedies began many years ago when I picked up the book *Healing Wise (Wise Woman Herbal)* by Susan Weed from Woodstock, New York. This interest led me to taking a course through my local adult education classes in herbology, where I learned the healing properties of many herbs, what was safe, what was not, and how to make tinctures, salves, and poultices. I became absorbed in the subject and decided to take an extensive home-study course with Susan Weed. My children were young at the time, and, as Aratron teaches, I raised them with a combination of regular medicine and herbal remedies. For example, if they had an ear infection, I used the doctor-prescribed antibiotic, but if they had a cold with a stuffy nose, I never gave them cold medicine; instead, I added a few drops of eucalyptus essential oil to a pot of hot water, made a tent, and had them breathe in the vapors. This worked like a charm to clear up their stuffiness and always made them feel better. So balance and harmony are key. If you have interest in inviting Aratron into your life, quiet your mind, focus with sincerity, and call to him to connect you with the ancient knowledge of plants. Don't be surprised if you find yourself in just the right place, at just the right time, for just the right book, class, or mentor to present itself. When that happens, don't forget to smile and bid Aratron a big, sincere thank you.

The earth element is the basis and foundation of our physicality. Without earth's foundation, we would have no platform to spring forward from. Due to the elemental association of the zodiac signs, their angels work closely with the nature angels in all matters that relate to those elements. With regard to the earth element, there are three. Do you remember Nadiel, the angel of Capricorn, who helps overcome challenges, teaches you to see them as opportunities for growth, and helps you move steadily forward in your desired direction? Do you remember Tual, the angel of Taurus, who helps you to let go of what no longer serves your best interest and can also, once the path is cleared, help you to undoubtedly see where you're going? And then there's Hamaliel, angel of Virgo, who helps you to achieve and maintain a sense of well-being, expanding your personal horizons. These are all angels of earth signs who work alongside nature's earth angels. Call upon any of them for extra support while working with Ariel, Zuphlas, Sachluph, or Aratron.

Ariel also oversees the air element. This element is related to the breath of life and governs the movement and expansion of the physical, mental, emotional, and spiritual aspects of yourself. The air element carries the intention of your true desire and brings it into expression by first creating the space for mental activity to take place and then allowing thoughts to develop, creating a clear picture of your intended desire. With this clarity, the air element moves you toward the needed action for realizing your dreams. An imbalance of the air element is identified in overuse or underuse by excessive or lack of mental, physical, emotional, or spiritual expression and movement. If you are stumbling across blocks, whether identified or not, that are preventing you from moving forward in your desired direction, call to Ariel for help. You may also summon Ruhiel, guardian angel of the winds, to help blow away all that is blocking you from success. There may be old scripts or patterns that have an energetic hold on you. These old patterns, blocking your growth, can be eliminated in various ways, but if you choose to work with the nature angels, Ariel and Ruhiel can surely break through and clear the air from patterns no longer serving you and replace them with new, healthy patterns that will help you become the person you desire to be. The zodiac angels associated with the air element include Libra's Zuriel, who helps you find self-compassion, which frees you of personal judgment. This will help you balance your needs with the needs of others without becoming overwhelmed. Gemini's Ambriel can help you identify and integrate your desires while keeping you balanced and moving in a direction that is for your highest good. However, if you have any questions about priorities, call to Aquarius's Cambiel to put you on the right path, pointing you in the right direction for achieving all your goals.

The fire element is ruled by Archangel Uriel, and while movement is governed by Ariel's air, it's Uriel's fire that oversees the direction that movement takes. The fire element directs motivation, willpower, and energy levels, as well as being the force that drives our systems of digestion and metabolism. The fire element is related to our personal power and sense of self and is associated with the solar plexus chakra. Imbalance in this area is generally indicated by feelings of uneasiness and anxiety, or by lack of energy. Uriel can help re-establish your sense of personal power, bringing your energy back into balance. Someone with an overactive fire element, or too much "fire in the belly," so to speak, may exhibit characteristics of being power-hungry, manipulative, or verbally, mentally, or physically abusive. This person may seem antsy, unable to sit still, displaying an excess of energy. Those lacking in the fire element may experience mental confusion, depression, insecurity, anxiety, a slow metabolism, or digestive difficulties. Work with Uriel to help cleanse and purify your energy fields, removing blocks that are preventing you from living the life you deserve. Uriel and his fire element can help bring your sense of personal power, motivation, and drive back into a healthy balance.

If you need help being assertive while achieving your goals without being aggressive, Aries's fire element angel, Machidiel, is the one to call. Being assertive rather than aggressive depends on your level of self-confidence and feelings of self-reliance. Those who are assertive exhibit confidence in undertaking their tasks without experiencing insecurity. They might not always know where a task is leading, but they are not afraid to move forward despite the unknown. They can give direction to others without bullying and praise without jealousy. They have a sense of personal power that comes from within but shines effortlessly outward. Assertiveness comes from the strength derived from a healthy, balanced sense of self. However, aggressiveness is just the opposite and manifests through forceful, angry interactions, often stemming from a position of lack or judgment. Those who must show their power forcefully often lack self-confidence, judging others and themselves harshly. Leo's Verchiel can take the lead here, as this angel can help balance the overstimulated fire element that causes aggressiveness by burning away past hurts and disappointments, replacing the void with a sense of peace, comfort, and self-security.

Another fire element angel is Sagittarius's Adnachiel, who can then help you set tangible goals, providing the spark to expand your vision and create an image of your desired outcome. Once your goal is clearly envisioned, Adnachiel helps you to remain focused on the action needed with just the right balance and assertiveness to attain your goals.

Some blocks cannot be burned away and need a more nurturing approach to their releasing. This is where the water element comes in. Phuel, guardian angel of water, can help wash away blocks holding you back from attaining the success you desire. Phuel is a very nurturing angel and is especially helpful with those issues originating from deep-seated early childhood trauma or from emotional or karmic sources. Many of these blocks are not apparent to your conscious mind and create uncomfortable feelings that you often don't understand. Phuel possesses the ability to nurture and comfort while encouraging the release of blocks from programs and scripts no longer relevant to your life. Have you ever experienced a "good" cry—a cry that started out as an expression of sadness, hurt, or anger, but then when you were done crying and you wiped your eyes, you felt a little better? This was Phuel being with you, helping you to release through your tears the sadness, hurt, or anger you felt due to conscious or subconscious emotions. Sometimes that's all you need. Sometimes you need to go through this process many times, but have no fear of crying, because now you know that Phuel is guiding you.

The zodiac angels affiliated with the water element are Cancer's Muriel and Pisces's and Scorpio's Barakiel. Remember, Barakiel is guardian to two zodiac signs with different focuses. Muriel washes away any deeply rooted blocks that prevent you from accessing your intuition and accepting yourself as an intelligent, creative, highly capable person. Pisces's Barakiel washes away the subconscious need to remain connected to people, places, or things that cause you emotional distress, ultimately holding you back from living a life of fulfillment. Scorpio's Barakiel washes away the root-cause of your fears. Whether it's the fear of failure or the fear of success, these unfounded fears are replaced with the ability to take on new challenges with confidence.

Having an excess in the water element department may result in being an oversensitive person, whereas not maintaining a healthy emotional water balance could manifest in being rigid and irrational. Phuel and the zodiac water angels help to maintain a healthy emotional balance and provide you with an abundance of compassion and unconditional love.

To strengthen the power of each element while working with the associated angel, try taking your relaxation breaths at the beginning of your invocations before calling in your angels, using the breath energetically linked to that element. The specific elemental breathing methods are as follows:

Earth Breath:

❖ When working with earth angels, *breathe in and out through the nose.*

Water Breath:

❖ When working with water angels, *breathe in through the nose, out through the mouth.*

Fire Breath:

❖ When working with fire angels, *breathe in through the mouth, out through the nose.*

Air Breath:

❖ When working with air angels, *breathe in and out through the mouth.*

Using these breaths as you begin to relax will help you focus and clarify the intent of your requested assistance. Once you are ready to call upon your angel, you may begin to breathe in a way that is comfortable for you. Say, out loud or silently, your angel's name three times, and continue with the invocation as described in Chapter 3. To add strength to your connection to an elemental angel, after you are relaxed and begin your invocation, you may continue to breathe according to the element breath as you call to your angel. To do this, using the method above, you would inhale as you silently call your angel's name – pause as you call your angel's name a second time – and exhale as you call your angel a third time, then breathe normally as you continue with your angelic connection. If you would like to add an advanced technique as you invoke your angels, this method of sacred breathing will help to increase the intensity of your connection, however, it's not necessary for acquiring your connection to the angels. To begin, as you inhale and silently call your angel's name, place the tip of your tongue behind your front teeth - hold for a moment's pause; then exhale, placing the tip of your tongue behind your bottom teeth – pause again. Repeat the entire process two more times, then breath normally. This may take practice, but once you get it down, I'm sure you'll agree it was well worth the effort.

Planting Your Garden with the Nature Angels

Plant a garden with the help of the angels and see how beautifully it grows. If you've ever planted a garden, you know that there are a few important steps to take before you enjoy the fruits of your labor. First, you must decide what you would like to grow, and then choose the right location, the right time or season, and the right amount of sun. Second, you'll need to prepare the soil, clearing it of all rocks and debris. Third, when you are ready to sow your seeds, you'll need to make sure you are planting them at the proper depth and spacing. Nurturing by proper care, water, and fertilizer will keep your plants healthy. You must continuously eliminate weeds that appear so that the roots of your plants stay healthy and unencumbered by unwanted growth. What a beautiful garden you can create! Finally, after all your hard work, you enjoy the harvest. You can be sure the nature angels were there to help, even if you didn't realize it. Much like your vegetable or flower garden, so can the angels help you create the garden of your dreams.

Unlike working with the zodiac angel focus wheel on a major goal over an entire year, working with the nature angels in your garden is useful for smaller, incremental change that can be accomplished over a season. Your garden work can also be a useful tool for working through any stage of your zodiac focus wheel that you are having difficulty with. The following exercise helps you to create change with help from the nature angels. Give thought to each step and then jot down your thoughts here. There is also additional space in the "My Nature Angel Garden for Change" section at the back of the book for planting a second garden.

Exercise 24
My Nature Angel Garden for Change

❖ Step 1: Decide what you would like to grow in your garden of life. What is your desired outcome? Take some time to think about it and call upon Archangel Ariel or Sachluph if you need help choosing the right seeds to plant or need guidance in developing your garden in general. What are your dreams?

_____

_____

_____

_____

❖ Step 2: Prepare the soil where your seeds will grow. The soil relates to your body, and this step requires eating right, sleeping well, and exercising the body, mind, and soul. You are preparing yourself for great change to blossom. What steps do you personally need to do to create a strong foundation upon which your seeds will grow? If you need help with this, call upon Zuphlas.

_____

_____

_____

_____

❖ Step 3: When your soil is ready, it's time to plant the seeds by taking action steps to place each seed carefully in the soil you have prepared. If you need help during the process, call upon Archangel Uriel to light the fire of motivation under you. Lack of motivation has to do with decreased sense of personal power. Nurturing is extremely important here and includes being easy on yourself and appreciating the effort you are making. Note ways you are nurturing yourself, but if you are stuck here, Phuel is the angel to call, for you can be assured his assistance will be gentle and kind.

_____

_____

_____

_____

❖ Step 4: The changes you are making may begin small, like a seedling, but grow strong with proper nurturing. Once the seeds are planted, after you have nurtured the seedlings and watched them grow, the next step is possibly the most important step of all: eliminating the weeds. In your garden of life, the weeds consist of negative thoughts, self-judgments, or old scripts causing unhealthy patterns or habits. Call upon Ruhiel for help in blowing away the energy keeping you attached to those weeds. Pay attention to any new weeds you find growing in your garden, and catch them early; otherwise, they will definitely stunt your growth and strangle your roots.

❖ Step 5: Finally there comes the harvest and evaluation of your crop. Here is where you enjoy the fruits of your labor and congratulate yourself on your efforts! Then, with an objective eye and without self-judgment or being overly critical of yourself, evaluate your outcome. Did you reap the intended results? Is there something you could do differently? Having a hard time with this last step? Call to Aratron for help.

Keep in mind that with each stage of gardening comes its own set of needs, and these will change as the season moves forward through its cycles. It will be important to keep focused on the intended outcome when challenges arise. But you have many angels to guide you, so call upon them. They are very willing to help.

chapter 7

tips for working with your angels

Now that you have been introduced to several angels, you may wonder which angel you should work with first, or how to choose an angel to work with for any given situation. Of course, you may always call upon any of the angels for help at any time, but I found that in the beginning, it's best to work with one or both primary guardians. Your connection is strongest to your guardians, and not only are they here to help and protect you, but they also oversee all the work you do with other angels. Your guardians are your gatekeepers, the angels who will guide you on every problem or concern and will lead you to other angels through the process. Once you are comfortable with your guardian angels, you will want to call upon the particular angel or angels that address the source of your problem. For example, in addition to your birth and zodiac guardians, if your concern relates to lack of courage for speaking up in a situation that is bothering you, you may want to call to Camael for help finding your courage. Or, if you're having difficulty being inspired at work, you may want to ask Uriel to "spark" your vision with new ideas. You will find overlap in the type of help provided by the angels. More than one angel can help in most situations. This is because not everyone connects with each angel in the same manner or with the same intensity. Some will develop stronger relationships with certain angels, while others develop close relationships with other angels. There is no right or wrong to this, and is why many angels have the same attributes. Personally, I'm closest to Michael, Raphael, Camael, Nadiel, Zuphlas, and Phuel, but I also have good relationships with many other angels. So don't get stuck on whom to call because if your guardian angel has other ideas, you'll know.

Here are a few more tips to help maximize your angel sessions. When planning to work with your angels, set aside at least ten minutes of undisturbed time. This will allow enough time for you to enter a relaxed state, center yourself, invoke your angels, and receive your angelic messages. Of course, you may always choose to dedicate more time, but I suggest a minimum of ten minutes. Next, before you begin your session, it's best to know what you are going to ask your angels because the clearer your intent, the easier it will be to determine which angels to ask for assistance. It will also make the work you do with the angels more focused. If you are having trouble identifying your need, call one of your guardians for help. As mentioned previously, you will want to invoke your angels by saying their names three times. The power of three plays an integral role in the integration and foundation of your body, mind, and soul. So calling the angel's name three times provides a strong foundation for which to state your intention. Once you have invoked your angels and made your request, relax, enjoy, and know that the angels are immediately on task working on your behalf. Of course, don't forget to thank your angels. Lastly, get into the habit of writing down your experiences and date your entries. This will provide a record and timeline of your progress and hopefully will prove to be an enjoyable account of your developing relationships with the angels.

In today's fast-paced world, many people are overextended, overwhelmed, or overworked, all causing an incredible amount of stress. I especially notice an increasing amount of stress in the workplace causing conflict between coworkers. For this reason, the intent for the following exercise is a quick, ten-minute session to reduce stress due to workplace conflict. In this example, we'll use Friday's birth guardian, however, in your own practice and use, replace the guardian and concern with your own. You'll begin by calling to your primary guardian for help. It's also beneficial, but not necessary, to invite other angels whose attributes address the source of your stress. Together, these angels will work to help relieve your stress and regain balance and harmony in your life. If your guardian is the same angel that addresses your specific stress source, that's fine. But if not, you can call upon any or all the angels to help in your situation if you feel guided to.

Exercise 25
Reducing Stress in Ten Minutes

Before beginning, choose your primary guardian (*Haniel for Friday*). Next, determine which angel(s) best support your concerns (*Camael for the courage and personal power to speak up and Cassiel for instilling peace and harmony in the workplace*). Set up and, if needed, write down your request for assistance (*to reduce stress due to workplace conflict and to find the right words to deal with the situation in a calm, mature, and satisfying way*). Now you are ready to begin your ten-minute meditation.

❖ Begin with the opening protocol.
❖ "Haniel, Haniel Haniel, please be with me now and help me to reduce the stress I'm experiencing caused by the disagreement I had with my coworker. Please help me find the right words to solve the issue between me and [name of coworker] so that harmony can be restored in

the workplace and my stress over this situation can be relieved."

❖ "Camael, Camael, Camael, please with me now and give me the courage to speak up without hatred or judgment toward my coworker or myself, so that a reasonable solution to the problem can be achieved for the highest good of all concerned."

❖ "Cassiel, Cassiel, Cassiel, please be with me now and help bring peace and harmony to the situation and to my life in general."

❖ Remain relaxed; the angels will do the rest. (If your mind wanders, focus on your breath, counting silently to three as you inhale, holding for three counts, and then slowly counting to three as you exhale. Before you know it, you'll be back into a state of relaxation.)

❖ When ready, use the closing protocol.

Don't worry about feeling, hearing, seeing, or thinking anything; just allow yourself to be in the moment for as long as it feels comfortable. Then go about your day, and know that the angels are on the job! Nothing else needs to be done. You may feel an immediate reduction in your stress level, being inspired to say just the right thing to resolve your conflict. Or, within a day or two, you may find yourself having the perfect conversation with your coworker, one that brings clarity and resolution to the situation. Certainly, don't be surprised if you hear a song with words that bring an idea of a solution to mind, or if a solution seems to arise for you right out of thin air. The angels work in ways that are for our highest good, and no two people are alike. Let the angels do their work. All you have to do is to allow yourself to receive their messages and follow their loving guidance. You may use this exercise as often as you like and in all matters that concern you. It only takes ten minutes.

chapter 8

a special message from archangel raphael

While I was working on the second draft of this book, Raphael came to me in his usual tingling way. Once he got my attention, I kept hearing the word *meditation* through my inner ears. It was like Raphael was nudging me, urging me, almost to the point of being annoying (although I could never be annoyed with the angels). He kept at it and at it until I finally acknowledged what he was trying to convey. Raphael wanted me to write about meditation. However, I didn't understand because I had already written several meditations and explained the process. So I asked for clarity. Here is the communication between us.

Good morning, Raphael, I said silently to acknowledge his presence.

Through my "inner ears," I heard him respond, *Good morning*.

Then I excitedly said, *I'm working on my book, and I'm almost finished.*

Immediately the word *meditation* came through, and it came through repeatedly, *meditation, meditation, meditation*, I heard.

Meditation, meditation, meditation, he repeated.

Oh, meditation, I responded. *Is there something you want me to know about meditation?*

Again, Raphael said, *Meditation, meditation, meditation.* (Remember what I've said about repetitiveness? Well, this is a perfect example.)

Okay, I replied, *can you please clarify? What is it that you want me to know about meditation? Is it something you want me to add to the book?*

In my mind, I was still a bit confused because I had already addressed meditation in the book, but I never dismiss a message from the angels. So when Raphael, immediately following my last question about adding to the book, responded by downloading into my thoughts the word *affirmative,* I knew what I had to do.

Okay, I said, but before I had the chance to grab a pen and paper to write it all down, the message started to flow, and it was coming extremely fast. I had to ask Raphael to stop a minute so I could get what I needed, and then ask him to start again and to slow it down a bit. Through the process of automatic writing, this is what Raphael downloaded into my mind (unfiltered) and asked me to share.

> *Many know meditation as sitting in silence; some know not of meditation at all. It is important for you to explain to the student of meditation that there are three types of mediation to know at this time: passive, active, and guided. Passive meditation is the most subtle form of focused concentration, where through this concentration the student is brought to a place of quiet mind. This concentration may be placed on thought, breath, or an object seen and focused on with inner or outer eyes. The purpose of all meditation is to find inner peace, a calming feeling within—to relax and de-stress, as you would put it. Passive meditation also opens channels and allows space for receiving. It is often while you are in passive meditation that messages*

are received. The second form of meditation is guided meditation, which serves its purpose by guiding the meditator through a sequence of images to find a place of calm, peaceful being-ness. A superb tool for beginners, as pressure from fear of not doing it right is eliminated. This fear is one's ego-mind vested in controlling the body, mind, and spirit, keeping it spinning out of control and in stressfulness. Guided meditation is also useful and enjoyable to those of experienced practice. One may guide one's own meditation images through creation of one's mind-thoughts directed to a special place or scene of beauty and relaxation and go there any time one wishes. The third, active meditation, achieves tension release and tranquility as physical movement is employed, followed by stillness. Active meditation generates heat from within, releasing outward, dissolving tension energy, making space for stillness, allowing the meditator to enter a tranquil state of Oneness as the triad, body, mind, and soul, comes to its still point. In the silent stillness of this aligned centeredness, the pulse of one's own energy may be felt and higher vibrational messages may be received. You may be familiar with these examples of active meditation, among them yoga, tai chi, qi gong, and some forms of dance. Share this knowledge of three meditation types identified here now, allow the awareness of such practice into your hearts, and know these are also methods used to receive our messages. May meditation of any method bring everlasting opportunity for holding a space of peace, relaxation, calmness, and guidance within your precious life. This is the end for now.

Of course, I thanked Raphael for this information, and I would like to point out a couple of things. Did you notice that this communication came to me in different ways? I first received a clairsentient message letting me know that Raphael was with me. This came through as the tingling sensation I have come to associate with his presence. I then clairaudiently heard the word *meditation* repeatedly and responded with questions for clarification. Clarification was immediately received, again, clairaudiently. When it came to receiving the actual message Raphael wanted me to share, this came to me claircognizantly through the process of automatic writing. What is important to know is that communication with the angels may come to you in more than one way. Here, I received the majority of the message claircognizantly. This is because clear knowing is my strongest "clair," but I also have a strong clairsentient relationship with Raphael, and it's through the tingling sensation that I most easily recognize when he is with me. My clairaudient messages generally come as words heard through my inner ears, and while I clearly understood the word *meditation,* the message itself needed clarification. What is important to know here is that communication with the angels goes both ways. When you receive messages you don't understand, regardless of the method, always ask for clarification. You can do so out loud or silently, but don't be afraid to ask, and don't hesitate to keep asking for more and more clarification until you understand.

chapter 9

meditations with the angels

Here you will find three guided meditations designed to be used any time you need help relaxing, finding inner peace and tranquility, or regrouping from a particular uncomfortable situation. Read through them a couple of times to get the gist of the images; then close your eyes and visualize what you just read. Or you may record yourself reading the meditations, using your own recorded voice as the guide to the imagery. You may also play background music while recording your voice, but make sure the music is soft so that your words are clearly heard. Once you become comfortable with guided meditations, you may want to create your own meditations. There is no wrong way to craft your personalized meditation; just be creative and enjoy the process.

Each of the following meditations will begin with a prelude and end with an epilogue, which are similar to but much lengthier than the opening and closing protocols used with the exercises. The first meditation will bring in Archangel Gabriel's energy to help in any situation you need assistance with. It's a perfect meditation if you are having trouble determining which "clair" is easiest for you to develop, or if you want help to further strengthen your connection with one or all four "clairs." The particular request in this meditation will focus on releasing resistance to receiving and understanding messages from the angels, but you may substitute any concern you have, so if this is not a concern of yours, take a moment to give thought to what your focus will be. As you go through the meditation pause after each line giving yourself time to fully visualize each image, and if possible, try to feel as though you are actually there; part of the scene. This may take practice.

The Prelude

❖ Sit comfortably in a chair with feet flat on the floor and hands resting on your lap, palms facing up.

❖ Begin to take slow, deep breaths, and when you are ready, gently close your eyes.

❖ As you inhale, imagine a white light entering and filling your entire body with relaxation.

❖ As you exhale, imagine you are releasing all negativity and tension that is stored in your body. Feel it leave every cell of your body, dissolving into nothingness.

❖ Inhale white light of relaxation.

❖ Exhale negativity, tension, and resistance.

❖ Inhale white light.

❖ Exhale negativity and tension.

❖ Feel yourself begin to relax as you sink deeper and deeper into your chair.

❖ Release any remaining tension in your body until you feel completely relaxed.

❖ Now, while breathing normally, imagine you are in the middle of a beautiful, lush, green meadow.

❖ In the distance, you see a gate, and behind it, a wooden bench underneath a tall tree.

❖ You think to yourself that you would like to sit on this bench and rest awhile.

❖ As you enter the gate and walk toward the bench, you realize that you have been here before.

❖ This is your special bench, a place where you spend time with the angels.

❖ You walk over to the bench and sit down.

❖ It's so peaceful, and then you remember that you always feel good here.

❖ This is where you always find peace and tranquility.

❖ Look around and see the beautiful wildflowers in the meadow. The colors are vibrant and the fragrances so sweet.

❖ There is a nest of baby birds in a tree above.

❖ Hear them softly chirping, singing their new song.

❖ The sun is shining down on you. Look up and feel the warmth of the sun's rays on your face.

❖ Soak it all in, feeling the warmth surround your entire body.

❖ As you gaze upward, you notice a few fluffy, white clouds floating gracefully against the blue sky.

❖ As you sit on your bench, you begin to feel connected to nature in a magical way.

❖ You begin to imagine that your feet are rooted deeply into the ground, like the roots of a tree.

❖ Feel your roots grow down, deeper and deeper, all the way down until the roots of your tree reach the center of Mother Earth.

❖ Now imagine the branches and leaves of your tree rising up from your crown, going upward and outward.

❖ Feel them going up higher and higher into the sky, feeling yourself sitting up straighter and straighter.

❖ Imagine your branches going up so high they pass the white, fluffy clouds, going higher and higher.

❖ You are now connected to nature, from heaven to earth.

Meditation with Gabriel

❖ As you remain relaxed and connected, you notice that before you stands Archangel Gabriel, messenger angel of communication, guardian of Mondays, to moon energies, and guide to hopes and dreams.

❖ He stands in front of you with his silver light illuminating the sky.

❖ You ask Gabriel to help you release the resistance you have toward receiving and understanding your messages from the angels.

❖ You sit quietly as Gabriel slowly takes your hands and places them over your heart center.

❖ You feel the radiance of your own energy coming from your hands, and it feels warm and comforting.

❖ Gabriel then takes his hands and places them over your crown, sending a soft, silver light down into your crown and through to your heart center.

❖ You can feel your heart expanding even more, welling up with love.

❖ This expansion brings you a secure, peaceful feeling.

❖ You know you are feeling the love emanating from Gabriel, yet you feel as though you are part of that love, that you *are* love.

❖ Gabriel asks you to sit in stillness for a few minutes.

❖ You do as Gabriel asks, keeping your mind still.

❖ If it begins to wander, Gabriel says not to worry, but to bring it right back to your focus.

❖ Gabriel counsels, "Practice stilling your mind, freeing yourself of unnecessary chatter, as it is the stillness that promotes tranquility and calmness of heart, thus allowing such peaceful focus to then promote love."

❖ He continues, "Love can release and dissolve any resistance you hold, and this releasing provides a gentle opening for communication with the angels."

❖ Gabriel also tells you that above all, angelic support and guidance comes at the appropriate time and will always be for your highest good.

❖ Gabriel then sits with you on the bench for what seems a long time and assures you that you will be given the answers to your questions.

❖ You take some time to sit quietly with Gabriel, all the while feeling his love.

❖ He then rises and places a small silver heart in your hands.

❖ He tells you whenever you need to find your still point, to bring this to your heart center, quiet your mind, and breathe.

❖ Gabriel then turns to walk out of the meadow. As you watch, his image gets smaller and smaller, until he disappears over the horizon. As he does, you thank Gabriel and forever lock within you this experience by saying, "I accept this truth as part of me, sealed by love and light, love and light, love and light."

The Epilogue

❖ You now begin to become aware of your surroundings.

❖ All the beauty noticed before seems even more beautiful, colors more vibrant, aromas more fragrant.

❖ You are filled with love for all nature, for all life, including for yourself.

❖ You remain sitting for a while, enjoying the feeling of peacefulness on this glorious day.

❖ You feel open, clear, and happy.

❖ It's now time to leave your meadow and go back home.

❖ You take a slow, deep breath as you retract the roots and branches of your tree.

❖ Take a moment to center yourself.

❖ Then slowly rise up from your bench and begin to walk back toward the gate.

❖ But as you walk away, you turn slightly to look once more.

❖ You smile to yourself because you know that you can come here anytime you need to find peace within, or anytime you want to call upon the help of the angels.

❖ You continue walking until you reach the gate of your meadow, and as you walk through, you close the gate firmly behind you.

❖ As you take a slow, deep breath, gently bring your attention back into the room.

❖ When you are ready, slowly open your eyes and look around the room. Wiggle your fingers and toes, and drink a glass of water.

The second meditation is with Archangel Michael, the angel of strength and protection. This meditation is for removing blockages from old scripts that are holding you back from success or happiness of any kind. As with any meditation, you may tailor it to your specific concerns.

Meditation with Michael

❖ Begin with the prelude.

❖ As you sit there on your bench, enjoying these moments, taking in all the beautiful sights, sounds, and smells, you notice in the distance a large, majestic figure.

❖ You sit there in awe as he slowly comes toward you.

❖ You see he is wearing a royal blue cloak and holds a round shield and mighty sword.

❖ You immediately know this is Archangel Michael, one of the Sacred Seven, the angel of strength and protection, so you feel perfectly safe.

❖ Now standing directly in front of you, Archangel Michael holds out his hand to you.

❖ As you place your hand in his, you slowly come to a standing position.

❖ You ask Michael to help you remove the blockages from old scripts you carry around within you.

❖ You may describe a particular situation, but you don't have to, because Michael knows what you need.

❖ Archangel Michael now stands to your left side, raising his mighty sword.

❖ As he points the tip toward your crown, the sword turns into a beautiful flower vase filled with golden liquid light.

❖ As he begins to pour the golden liquid light into your crown chakra, he says to you, "With the power of my golden ray of pure light, all old, painful experiences and the scripts and patterns resulting are washed away. All blocks preventing success and happiness are removed from this point forward."

❖ As you stand taking in the golden liquid light, you can feel the light cleanse your crown chakra, washing away and releasing any blockages that might reside there.

❖ You now feel the golden liquid light as it moves down into the area between your eyes and cleanses your third eye chakra, washing away and releasing any blockages that might reside there.

❖ Feel the golden liquid light as it moves down into your throat area and cleanses your throat chakra, washing away and releasing any blockages that might reside there.

❖ Feel the golden liquid light as it moves down into your heart area and cleanses your heart chakra, washing away and releasing any blockages that might reside there.

❖ Feel the golden liquid light as it moves down into the area of your solar plexus and cleanses your solar chakra, washing away and releasing any blockages that might reside there.

❖ Feel the golden liquid light as it moves down into your lower abdomen area and cleanses your sacral chakra, washing away and releasing any blockages that might reside there.

❖ Feel the golden liquid light as it moves down into the base of your spine area and cleanses your root chakra, washing away and releasing any blockages that might reside there.

❖ When the golden liquid light has passed through each of your chakras, you repeat Michael's words, as an affirmation and you say, "With the power of Michael's golden ray of pure light—my old painful experiences and the scripts and patters resulting—are washed away.—All blocks preventing my success and happiness are removed—from this point forward."

❖ Michael tells you that you can call upon him whenever you feel the need to eliminate old patterns no longer serving you.

❖ You thank Michael and forever lock within you this experience by saying, "I accept this truth as part of me, sealed by love and light, love and light, love and light."

❖ He touches your forehead gently and then disappears into the sunlight.

❖ Finish with the epilogue.

The third meditation is with Scorpio's Barakiel. Barakiel supports us in making the right decisions by helping us to evaluate our goals and attain our true potential.

Meditation with Barakiel

❖ Begin with the prelude.

❖ Your head begins to tilt back slightly as you open your eyes and notice the white, fluffy clouds in the sky are changing shape.

❖ You watch closely as they gracefully dance across the sky, moving forward and backward and up and down, forming different shapes along the way.

❖ Take a moment to identify what shapes you see.

❖ Now you notice that all these white, fluffy clouds are starting to join together.

❖ They are forming one big shape, the shape of an angel.

❖ Before you, up in the sky, you see a beautiful angel with wings and a flowing white robe.

❖ Then out of the sky comes an angel to sit with you on your special bench.

❖ The angel tells you he is Barakiel, the angel of the zodiac, Scorpio.

❖ He tells you he is here at your request to help you realize your true potential.

❖ Yes, you remember you called upon Barakiel to help you with your important decision.

❖ You are happy he is with you, and you feel completely safe and at ease.

❖ Barakiel tells you he will help you find your still point, the place of perfect peace, where your heart will guide you in making important decisions about your future.

❖ He asks you to take a moment to mold the decisions you need help with into a ball, and to then hand the ball to him for holding.

❖ Next, Barakiel asks you to imagine you are placing your ego behind you, so that your extraneous thoughts don't interfere with your mind or heart.

❖ Holding your decisions in his hands, Barakiel tells you he will help you to evaluate your situation.

❖ He then asks you to breathe in and out the color red.

❖ And as you do, Barakiel says: "With the color vibration of red expanding your root chakra, you have the energy and vitality you need to recognize and move forward with the true nature of your decision."

❖ Next, breathe in and out the color orange.

❖ And as you do, Barakiel says: "With the color vibration of orange within your sacral chakra, you have the opportunity to create change and life transformation."

❖ Breathe in and out the color yellow.

❖ "With the color vibration of yellow within your solar chakra, you have the personal power and self-confidence to trust your judgment."

❖ Breathe in and out the color green into the heart area and then pink into this same area.

❖ Blend the two colors, green and pink, to inhale and exhale the color magenta.

❖ "With the color vibration of magenta within your heart chakra, you find your heart's desire, as it is the intent of your true self, in all its positive aspects, for your life to move forward in this direction."

❖ Now inhale and exhale the color light blue.

❖ "With the color vibration of light blue within your throat chakra, you find ways to express your new heart's desire."

❖ Next, inhale and exhale the color indigo or dark blue.

❖ "With the color vibration of indigo within your third eye chakra, you are able to imagine and see yourself living your new heart's desire."

❖ Now, inhale and exhale the color violet.

❖ "With the color vibration of violet within your crown chakra, you have the angels surrounding and supporting you in your new heart's desire."

❖ Barakiel takes your newly transformed desire, which he still holds, and carries it high up into the sky.

❖ From his hand, he pours not just the sparkles of your new heart's desire, but also the realization of your potential for moving forward on your new path.

❖ And as you look up and see these sparkles gracing the sky like nighttime twinkling stars—you take a moment to absorb it all.

❖ Then you realize you have found the answers to your questions.

❖ And even though you know there may come a time when you have questions again, you are comforted to know that Barakiel holds the sparkles of your new desires and will always guide you, if you just ask.

❖ As Barakiel blends into the clouds and disappears into the blue sky, you thank him and forever lock within you this experience by saying, "I accept this truth as part of me, sealed by love and light, love and light, love and light."

❖ Finish with the epilogue.

chapter 10

a special message from archangel raziel

During the writing of this book, my brother-in-law passed away. He lost his battle to cancer. Even though his death was not sudden, it was, nonetheless, a difficult time for my sister and our family. Arrangements were made to take the eight-hour drive with my eighty-four-year-old parents to my sister's home. That very same day, I began receiving messages from an angel I had not yet developed a relationship with. His name is Archangel Raziel. I kept hearing his name over and over again, clairaudiently (through my inner ears), and so I looked him up to find that Raziel is the angel of ancient wisdom and mystery. *Hmm, interesting*, I thought. Not only did I keep hearing his name, but I also started feeling him around me, sensing his presence. Was there a message I needed to receive? Was it something I needed to pass on to my sister? I kept wondering, and I kept asking. I receive a lot of my messages in the shower. I attribute this to my close relationship with Phuel, the angel of water. So I asked Phuel for help, and when I did, I immediately got my answer. (Thank you, Phuel!) The message was meant not only for my sister, although it came at a most appropriate time, but also for me, and for you too, through the writing of this book. So, I started communication with Raziel.

Before I share his message, I need to preface it with the story I told my sister on the day of her husband's burial before I shared this same message with her. "Imagine this," I told her. "When a fetus is in its mother's womb, it lives in the only world it knows. It floats around and is content sucking its thumb in the only world it knows, its mother's womb. Here, the fetus is nourished, comforted, and loved, and it can't imagine any other existence. In the world of its mother's womb, the fetus is very happy. Then one day, it's time to leave the womb, and the baby is born, entering a world that he had no idea existed when he was in his mother's womb. He had no concept of this new world until he left the womb and was born. Here he is nourished, comforted, and surrounded by people who love him and care for him. He lives a life here on earth and is very happy because he knows nothing else. He has no concept that anything else exists beyond earth. Then one day, it's time to leave earth, and he is born into an even greater world, one that he had no previous concept of existed. He couldn't even imagine the beauty, peace, joy, love, and comfort that he finds now. Here, in Heaven, the angels surround him and wrap their soft wings around him to comfort him and keep him warm. There are loved ones he once knew to greet him and to love him and to share in his experience. And he is very happy in his new world." My sister listened intently and with tears in her eyes as I continued and told her that Archangel Raziel, angel of wisdom and mystery, gave me the following message to share with her (and all of you). I received this message through claircognizance (unfiltered).

> *When a person leaves the physical body and crosses into the new world of energetic form, he or she is first met by the energy of loved ones who have passed before him or her. There is a signature energy, a signature vibration of those who have previously incarnated together, a group*

signature that the loved one who just crossed over must integrate and blend with. In order to help with this process, these signature energies take on any form that is needed for the newly departed to recognize and feel safe with them, such as the form of previously departed loved ones. Their job is to assist the newly departed and help him or her assimilate into the signature energy group, which is part of the collective energy of the All, and help those left behind heal. What this means to those remaining is that when a person first loses a loved one and has thoughts, feelings, or a knowing that the loved one is near, that person is actually receiving the message of love from his or her entire signature group. Not only is the person feeling the energy of the newly departed loved one, but he or she is also receiving love and comfort from the energies of all the relatives and loved ones belonging to that particular signature energy group. Collectively the signature energy group comes to aid the healing of broken hearts, as you would call it. The aid comes in the form of pure unconditional love transmissions of the highest. Each time the departed loved one is brought to mind, these transmissions are taking place. And so is the mystery revealed.

It may be a difficult concept to understand, but when I told my sister this, explaining that her husband is now part of the collective energy group shared with his mother and all those who have ever loved him, and that when she has a thought of her husband, she is actually sensing the presence, love, and comfort of all of them, my sister felt peace and comfort within her heart, at least in that moment.

Whether it be the day of a funeral or years later, we are constantly receiving messages of love energy sent by our deceased loved ones, which are the blended energies of all our loved ones, and part of the Oneness of All. If you feel it, embrace those transmissions of pure unconditional love from above.

Thank you, Raziel, for coming to me and helping my sister and all others who do or eventually will, understand this important message.

chapter 11

and in the end

The angels want you to remember that love comforts, love heals, love protects, and love knows no boundaries. Don't be afraid to ask the angels for help. They are here for the purpose of helping us to grow, be happy, and experience love and joy. Love is the vibration of angels. The angels emanate at the highest frequency, which is pure, divine love. When you express love toward someone, you radiate the vibration held at the angelic frequency level. This originates from the center of your heart, your soul, and core being. It is expressed vibrationally and expands outward in all directions. This expanded energy, in turn, like a magnet, attracts and pulls toward you "like" vibrations.

These like vibrations may not manifest immediately, but by maintaining a consistent level of unconditional love in your heart, even in the midst of difficult times (ask the angels to help you with this), you are certain to experience the joys of love received. This will happen at different times for different people, but know that in the right time, with the right person, the right situations will unfold, and you will be on the receiving end. Watch for signs and embrace them. Allow yourself to be open to receive love, which, for some, is more difficult than giving love. Ask the angels for assistance.

You may call upon specific angels for help and develop one, some, or all of your "clairs" to strengthen your relationship and receptiveness to angel messages. This book gives you the opportunity to begin this process. Don't worry about mastering everything all at once. Building a relationship with the angels is similar to building a friendship. Every friendship starts with a simple introduction, such as "Hello, my name is ..." and your friendship with the angels can start that same way. As people spend more time together getting to know each other, their relationship grows, and you will find the same is true as you develop your relationship with the angels. In life, we are lucky if we find one true friend whom we can depend on through thick or thin. With the angels, you will have many true friends that love you and will be there for you any time you're in need. Picking up this book is a sign from the angels that you are ready. Take this opportunity to introduce yourself and get acquainted. Begin to spend time with the angels and practice the exercises and mediations in this book. As you do, you will be strengthening your relationship and will find that as time goes on, it will become easier and easier to recognize and interpret angelic messages. That will make the angels very happy.

As I came toward the end of writing this book, I gave considerable thought to the best way of summing up what the angels wanted me to convey. During this process, I reviewed my own life experiences and the role angels have played in my growth and development. I went through a humble soul-search to find what has made me the person I am today; so blessed with angel love. What I found was that although I didn't always know it, the angels have been most instrumental in my development right from the very beginning. They have been my protectors and my guides, have given me strength, helped me heal, shown me compassion, and taught me tolerance. They have directed me toward a life infused with a love of all sentient life, a soul that feels the music and dances to that feeling. I am truly grateful for all my blessings, but I realize my growth didn't happen overnight. Messages from the angels sometimes come in strange ways, and it's important to remain open and allow yourself to absorb the vibrations, even if you don't understand the messages at the time. It may just be that the angels are planting seeds for a later harvest. Such was the case with me.

Being a child of the sixties and growing up with the British invasion rocking and rolling the youth of America, I spent much of my pre- and early teenage years listening to the music of the Beatles. Little did I realize that some of their lyrics would have a profound effect on my life (but of course, the angels knew). As I listened to countless hours of Beatles, singing along about love and peace and "flying into the light of the dark black night," (okay, "Blackbird" was one of my favorites), I truly felt the love, truly felt the peace. As for sending light into darkness, well, I wouldn't understand that message until much later in life. As I was contemplating how to summarize my points for this last chapter, a line from a Beatles song that I hadn't heard in decades came to mind. It wasn't just a fleeting thought; the angels downloaded this line into my mind, and just like a tune you can't get out of your head, I kept hearing, through my inner ears, these words over and over and over again until I finally realized the angels were sending me the ending of this book. Ironically, the name of the song is "The End," and the words I kept hearing were "And in the end, the love you take is equal to the love you make." It became ever so clear to me in completing this work that the angels wanted you to know that in the end, the bottom line is that "Everything is love, and love is everything. And it is within the field of love that you find peace and tranquility. It is within the field of love that all positive change is made possible. In other words, the love you make is so equal to the love you take."

I invite you to develop a relationship with the angels. I ask that you to take from this book what helps you and leave what doesn't, but always know that the angels love you. May the love and light of angel sparkles be forever within your heart.

The end

yet just the
beginning.

my personal
angel dictionary

List words, colors, numbers, sounds, and repetitions
here with their associated meanings for you.

My Personal Angel Dictionary

An account of the special language I share with the Angels.

A

_____

_____

_____

_____

B

_____

_____

_____

_____

C

_____

_____

_____

_____

D

_____

_____

_____

_____

E

F

G

H

I

J

K

L

M

N

O

P

Q

R

S

T

U

V

W

X

Y

Z

my zodiac angel focus wheel for change

My Zodiac Angel Focus Wheel for Change

Month and Day/Beginning Angel:_____

(See chapter 5.)

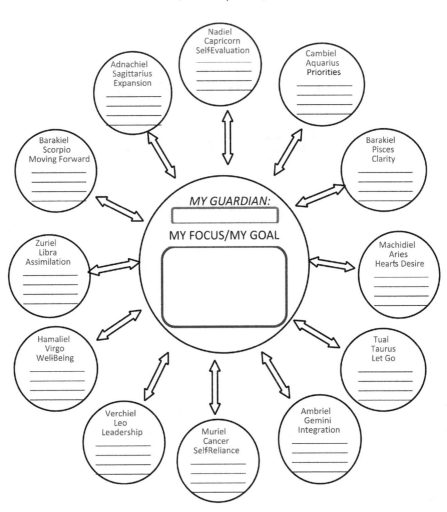

OUTCOME:

My Zodiac Angel Focus Wheel for Change

Beginning Month and Day/Angel:_____

(See chapter 5.)

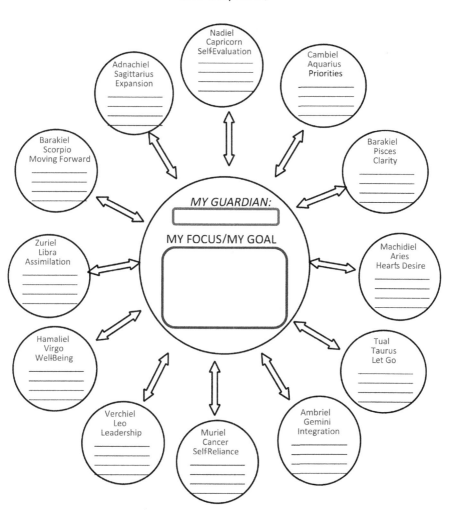

OUTCOME:

my nature angel

garden for change

Record the steps as you plant your garden.

(See chapter 6.)

My Nature Angel Garden for Change

❖ Step 1 (Ariel and Sachluph): Decide what you would like to grow in your garden of life. What are your dreams?

_____

_____

_____

_____

_____

_____

_____

_____

❖ Step 2 (Zuphlas): Prepare the soil where your seeds will grow. In what ways do you ready yourself for change?

_____

_____

_____

_____

_____

_____

_____

❖ Step 3 (Uriel and Phuel): Planting and nurturing your seeds. What action steps do you take in planting your seeds, and how do you nurture yourself once they are planted?

_____

_____

_____

_____

_____

_____

_____

_____

❖ Step 4 (Ruhiel): As your seedlings sprout and your plants grow you will find unwanted weeds surfacing. List some ways you will keep your garden healthy and free of weeds.

_____

_____

_____

_____

_____

_____

_____

_____

_____

_____

❖ Step 5 (Ariel and Aratron): The harvest and evaluation. Are you satisfied with the yield? Did your garden grow the way you had hoped? Try to be objective and note what worked, what needed more attention, and what you might do differently the next time you plant your garden.

_____

_____

_____

_____

_____

_____

_____

_____

_____

_____

List any other notes about your experience
with your "Garden for Change" here.

_____

_____

_____

_____

_____

_____

_____

_____

_____

_____

my personal
angel journal

Write notes here from
exercises, meditations, or any angel experiences you have.

Date:_____ To: _____

My Personal Angel Journal

My Personal Angel Journal

My Personal Angel Journal

My Personal Angel Journal

My Personal Angel Journal

My Personal Angel Journal

My Personal Angel Journal

My Personal Angel Journal

My Personal Angel Journal

My Personal Angel Journal

My Personal Angel Journal

My Personal Angel Journal

My Personal Angel Journal

My Personal Angel Journal

My Personal Angel Journal

My Personal Angel Journal

My Personal Angel Journal

My Personal Angel Journal

My Personal Angel Journal

My Personal Angel Journal

My Personal Angel Journal

My Personal Angel Journal

My Personal Angel Journal

My Personal Angel Journal

My Personal Angel Journal

about the author

Pamela Landolt is an energy healer and teacher who brings the angels into the lives of those who want to know them. Her journey began over 30 years ago when she was guided by an "inner voice" to seek alternative care for the management of her 1 ½-year-old baby boy's life-threatening food allergies. Unbeknownst to her, the guidance she received was that of the angels, and it led her to homeopathy, a holistic healing system which stimulates a person's natural healing powers. This started her on a lifelong adventure into the world of natural healing, and the angels have guided her along the way.

Pamela began her formal study of energy healing at the Polarity Institute in Watertown, MA, receiving Registered Polarity Practitioner status in 1998. She also holds a Masters in Metaphysics from the University of Metaphysics, and studied at Hands of Serenity Healing in Fishkill, NY achieving Usui Shuiki Ryoho Second Degree Reiki level. She is a Certified Angel Card Reader™ through Doreen Virtue's program, and in 2017 received certification as a Bio-Energy Field Transmitter from the Institute of Divine Potential.

Pamela is dedicated to spreading Love and Light to the world, and it is through her work as an author and healer that countless people have been touched by the angels and are living happier, healthier lives. She offers classes in Communing with the Angels, conducts angel healing sessions, Angel Card Readings, and as a Certified Bio-Energy Transmitter, leads group and individual sessions on reducing stress utilizing specialized bio-energy codes and techniques.

All of Pamela's work is guided by the angels, and she wishes to share their life-changing energy with you.

For more information visit www.Discovering-Angels.com.

index

U

Uriel 74, 75, 80, 83, 126

V

Verchiel 55, 56, 75
Virgo 56, 73

W

Water (element) 24, 34, 68, 69, 73,
    74, 75, 76, 77, 78, 79, 96, 103
Well-being 56, 57, 73

Z

Zadkiel 11, 43
Zodiac guardian 45, 46, 47, 48, 50,
    53, 54, 55, 56, 57, 58, 59, 61,
    62, 64, 83
Zuphlas 69, 70, 71, 73, 80, 84, 126
Zuriel 57, 58, 62, 63, 74

Printed in the United States
By Bookmasters